If you want to build trust, maximize discretionary effort, and develop talent, read this book. It provides a proven toolset that moves the needle in the key areas that produce competitive advantage and does this across multiple cultures and countries. The book powerfully challenges conventional wisdom in many ways and is full of relatable insights into how to build trust through unconditional recognition, engagement, and by merging coaching and lean. I need this book in Mandarin Chinese for all my leaders!

—**Wayne Chin,** President, PECL, Taiwan

Provides a practical approach to engaging employees in the lean journey. A successful implementation of a lean culture depends on the leadership team's ability to drive the "why," and Frank's RME approach does this from the bottom-up. Frank's unique storytelling ability makes this book an enjoyable and easy read.

—**Eric Chan,** formerly Senior Lean Leader Americas at
GE Power Conversion

I really enjoyed the book. RME operating system (OS) can be applied to all businesses, and I would even say to governments. It outlines the importance of use of data to take subjectivity out of the process and engages the entire organization bottom-up and top-down to solve the key challenges facing organizations today.

—**Bill Henry,** President and CEO, HENRY SSS LLC, and formerly Principal Vice President, Bechtel Corporation

In order to sustain success in our world of continuous improvement, you must have culture and engagement. I love how Frank ties the importance of trust, even referring to it as fragile, to leadership and accountability. This really sets the stage for an employee-owned culture.

—**Rebecca Siers,** Senior Lean Director, STERIS Corporation

Factories and companies exist in the real world with real people. Frank has lived and breathed the real world of engagement for 40 years and he shares here his approach, stories, and humor (and some rather important models) to show how leadership humility and a belief in people can achieve amazing outcomes for everyone involved.

—**Rob Lewis,** Divisional Chief Executive, Halma

Every executive should read this book! Not for the faint-hearted but for courageous leaders serious about transforming their organizations via their people, it provides a practical and proven approach that has been adapted to local culture and circumstances across many sectors. I loved the storytelling, easy-to-read style combined with powerful and relatable examples throughout. Frank demonstrates that creating genuine employee pull for continuous improvement is so much better than the more traditional top-down approach.

—**Steve Howard,** Operations Manager, USA

Frank Devine cares deeply about making businesses and the individuals in them leaps and bounds better than they are today. His modeled approach is based on science, experience, and a profound (and proven) belief that organizational culture change that leads to significant step changes in performance is created more rapidly, not from leadership, but by the employees themselves.

—**Mike Mattingly,** Human Resources Director,
Nipro PharmaPackaging Americas

I am intrigued by the Consensus Day concept with total transparency and equality. This could be a game-changer.

—**Julie Nielson,** Director, Operations FTO, Amgen Corporation

Rapid Mass Engagement provides practical guidance on building long-lasting company culture and leadership. Frank offers a number of simple actions that every employer can take to achieve the unimaginable. I have seen many great initiatives that do not quite work, but the Rapid Mass Engagement method works simply because it engages every employee, and it is not imposed from the top.

 —Barbara Opala, Head of Legal, Norton Motorcyles

Frank has captured the key fundamentals of creating maximum value (to the individual and company) through full engagement of the most underutilized asset.

 —Arthur Leach, Vice President Operations, Activ Surgical

The book provides a roadmap to employee motivation through empowerment and the pursuit of a higher purpose.

 —Kamilia Sofia, Corporate Director, Atomic Energy of Canada

Rapid
Mass
Engagement

Rapid
Mass
Engagement

Driving Continuous Improvement Through Employee Culture Creation

Frank Devine

Mc
Graw
Hill

New York Chicago San Francisco Athens London Madrid
Mexico City Milan New Delhi Singapore Sydney Toronto

1 2 3 4 5 6 7 8 9   LCR   28 27 26 25 24 23

ISBN   978-1-264-73901-1
MHID   1-264-73901-X

e-ISBN   978-1-264-74080-2
e-MHID   1-264-74080-8

McGraw Hill books are available at special quantity discounts to use as premiums and sales promotions or for use in corporate training programs. To contact a representative, please visit the Contact Us pages at www.mhprofessional.com.

McGraw Hill is committed to making our products accessible to all learners. To learn more about the available support and accommodations we offer, please contact us at accessibility@mheducation.com. We also participate in the Access Text Network (www.accesstext.org), and ATN members may submit requests through ATN.

For Sally Devine (1925–2011) of Belturbet in County Cavan,
Ireland, and her father, Joe Devine (1889–1969) of Aughnacloy,
County Tyrone, whose love, example, and fortitude inspired this book.

Contents

Acknowledgments

*We had all the Lean processes, but it wasn't enough;
until we adopted the Rapid Mass Engagement
process to create the new culture, we were
getting frustrated and going nowhere.*

James Winters
VP Manufacturing, DePuy Synthes (Johnson & Johnson)
Orthopaedics Worldwide, commenting on the
Ringaskiddy site winning the Shingo Prize

In remembrance, I would like to thank David Bucknall of Rider Levett Bucknall and Tom McCarthy of Bechtel, whose insights would have improved this book had they lived to formally contribute to it. Both were superb, values-driven leaders who have left a powerful legacy in their organizations and beyond. You are missed, guys, and I hope you can hear this from wherever your energetic and kind spirits reside.

HN Shrinivas of Tata Hotels provided eye-witness testimony to how Ratan Tata's instruction that "we must reach out and care for every weeping eye" transformed the lives of the families of the deceased and injured after the terrorist attack on Mumbai. Thank you Ratan and Shrini for what you did; this book will be a success if it inspires others to follow your example.

Thank you also to John Bicheno for inviting me to join the founding group of guest lecturers in Cardiff's Lean Enterprise Research Council's MSc program in 2000, to Kate Mackle of the Kaizen Institute who recommended my approach to creating employee "Pull for Improvement" to LERC, and to all the MSc students who tested the conceptual and implementation framework outlined in these pages, first in the classroom and later in their multiple organizations.

Thank you also to the many thousands of employees who created the ever-increasing sample size of people using the concepts and skills explained in these pages. The years of feedback from those practitioners have enriched this book. Rapid Mass Engagement (henceforth RME) has facilitated tens of thousands of nonmanagement employees to systematically make decisions usually confined to senior management, decisions they would never have believed possible. In doing so these employees have tested and improved the RME concepts and skills. In this way "the voice of the customer" of leadership has spoken powerfully, helping to develop and test the concepts in innumerable practical ways, many out of reach of conventional research methods.

The sample size foundation of this work grows over time; when the case study sample size was small, it took real courage and trust in me and the process for the leaders to choose the most radical and, for them, most dangerous option available. John Speirs of Bacardi-Martini, Richard Davies and Steve Adams of Coca-Cola, Trevor Orman, Mike Moran, and Sue Savage of Rolls-Royce, Chris Reed and Mike Hood of Textron, Olof Faxander of Outokumpu, and the late David Bucknall and Ann Bentley of Rider Levett Bucknall did not have the comfort of many successful previous examples of RME when they risked their reputations by adopting it for their organizations. Yet they had the courage and integrity to back a process that tests (sometimes to destruction) the skills and values of the senior teams involved.

The ability to scale RME beyond previous workforce sizes is not a given. In 2015, James Lyons, Mike Flynn, Colm Shiels, and their colleagues in Boston Scientific did not have a previous example of RME in a site with 3,200 employees to guide their plan. Similarly, John Lynch, James Winters, and Cathal O'Reilly of DePuy lacked a similarly sized implementation before embarking on their transformation of the Ringaskiddy site in 2008.

Anthony Collins of Topflight did not have a reference business that had applied the RME philosophy across multiple sites and cultures with all the transitory employment and other challenges inherent in the travel sector; nor had he evidence of one that had grown through two separate recessions, yet he put his big heart, soul, and intellect into testing it in combat. Thank you also to Steve Long in GKN for volunteering his site to be the pilot for the distinctive leadership approach outlined in these pages and Pete Watkins for adopting and championing this material for global lean programs in GKN and elsewhere.

Having a local and employee-credible Higher Purpose is critical in RME. Higher Purpose is defined as having a more meaningful reason to work even than one experienced with purpose. Individuals, teams, and organizations can all have a Higher Purpose. Usually, the Higher Purpose is agreed on by the senior team. In contrast, Sean Coughlan and Andrew Cromie of ICBF and Colin Denman of Promed seized the advantage of small size to create their Higher Purpose in one day with their entire workforce.

Other individuals also played major roles in producing the outcomes detailed here. There are too many to mention, but my life has been enhanced working with wonderful leaders such as Siobhan Hopper, Ses Ardabili, Gavin Mitchell, Padraig Garvey, Mary Madden, Keith Allen, Catherine Healy, Dareena Melly, Gretta Collins, John Reidy, Enda Colleran, Eric Hennessy, Peter Gallagher, Aidus Curran, Barry O'Driscoll, Susan O'Halloran, Robbie Walsh, Maria Shanahan, Norman Black, Geoff Roche, Sheila Gallagher, Mike Cox, Chris Thomson, John Keogh, Donal Moloney, Steve Thorpe, Mark Ebdon, Donna Roche, Tony Cox, John Harris, Noel Hennessy, Jackie Cullen, Ian Forrester, Darren Tierney, Peter Smith, and Pete Hewitt.

Thank you to people from 82 organizations who have selflessly given interviews for this book at a time when their calendars were heavily populated with issues much more important than helping me. Their insights and data give readers access to diverse voices and interpretations way beyond what I could have provided on my own.

Finally, thank you to Glynis Caulfield, whose unrelenting selfless encouragement to write this book, and fearless and patient feedback through many drafts, made for a better initial manuscript, and thank you also to my editor, Judith Newlin, whose faith in the book made it possible and whose feedback, along with that of her colleague Jonathan Sperling, converted the manuscript into the better book you read today.

Introduction

Key Challenge for Senior Leaders

On June 12, 2022, London's *Sunday Times* reported that "the Bank of England has handed a contract worth £203,000 to [a certain] consultancy. The remit is to help 'define the essence' of the organization and explain why people should be proud and motivated to work for the Bank" (Chambers, Prufock diary section, *London Sunday Times*, 2022).

The conventional assumption that employees need this "explained" to them by a consultancy, top down, will be vigorously contested in this book. In September 2021, the *McKinsey Quarterly* warned:

> By not understanding what their employees are running from, and what they might gravitate to, company leaders are putting their very businesses at risk. Moreover, because many employers are handling the situation similarly—failing to invest in a more fulfilling employee experience and failing to meet new demands for autonomy and flexibility at work—some employees are deliberately choosing to withdraw entirely from traditional forms of full-time employment. (De Smet et al. 2021)

Let's address that challenge now. Senior leaders frequently express how difficult it is to succeed with "culture change" with top-down initiatives to create a competitive culture. This book provides an

1

alternative approach to achieving culture change, asking, "Why launch culture-change initiatives *top-down*, when a wide and deep employee commitment to such a culture can be created far quicker and more sustainably by the employees themselves?"

Having created this bottom-up energy and commitment, management is liberated to focus on nourishing and supporting that employee-created culture. This book is the story of how a laser focus on Higher Purpose and the rapid and mass engagement of employees has moved the dial for organizations of all types, improving key metrics, delivering organizational breakthroughs, increasing social mobility, and creating jobs in many organizations of all types.

The bottom-up process that delivers these results is called Rapid Mass Engagement (RME). RME both disrupts conventional thinking and simultaneously integrates diverse and previously disaggregated disciplines.

This is not just a book about leadership, engagement, or Continuous Improvement;* it is about how to leverage all three to meet your organization's goals. It provides data and testimony from many senior leaders on how RME helped achieve extraordinary results, such as:

- A 108 percent increase in jobs during the 2008–2010 recession while simultaneously increasing productivity
- A 90.5 percent increase in customer Net Promoter Score (NPS) to four times higher than large global brands in the sector
- A 30 percent reduction in working capital within six months (see Chapter 1)

---

* A note on terminology: I am using the term *Continuous Improvement* throughout to denote the entire body of knowledge variously known as lean, kaizen, Six Sigma, operational excellence, and agile, and all the derivative combinations that have emerged. That body of knowledge has been disaggregated and reaggregated over time with the creation of new, overlapping, and unhelpful terminology to create wasteful complexity for the practitioner. See Chapter 7 for further discussion.

I will explain how leveraging a radical form of mass employee engagement, a leadership approach to support it, and Continuous Improvement expertise changes culture and delivers competitiveness. You will be able to see how this occurs much quicker than conventional thinking argues is possible.

My aim is to provide a proven *integrated implementation mechanism* that delivers employees' yearning for purpose. In so doing it provides an alternative, win-win, socially impactful but commercially realistic approach to the social conflict and divisiveness that has become common in recent years.

These pages are also a practical manual for leaders, with Chapter 5 providing a step-by-step process overview and Chapter 12 summarizing all the key success factors needed to implement a radical, bottom-up, rapid and mass engagement of an entire workforce. I aim to make content memorable and practically useful when you need it, under pressure, in your organizations. In this pursuit, I have provided learning and framing deliberately widened beyond business and organizational life, including guest appearances by Donald Duck, King Lear, and Leonardo da Vinci.

Continuous Improvement's early manifestations in manufacturing gave many the impression that it is not relevant to services.* As services comprise a greater percentage of modern economies than manufacturing, and given the massive amount of non-value-adding activity in services, this is an unfortunate limiting assumption. I interviewed Donal Moloney, now global supply chain director for Abbott's Infectious Disease Division, on the transformation of DePuy Synthes's global supply chain following its RME in 2008. He explained how the various aspects of RME applied in a globally distributed services environment:

---

* The rapidly increased manufacturing output of the United States' Training Within Industry—inspired factories vastly outperformed both the Nazi and Soviet state-managed factories, a major factor in the outcome of World War II. This was a lesson Japan, particularly Toyota, learned better than the West in the postwar era.

The mass engagement process was an excellent fit with Johnson & Johnson's culture and with The Credo.* The mobilization of the entire organization at all levels delivered results quickly.

It provided a clear process for mobilizing our organization including the engagement of the entire workforce and ensuring the leaders had the knowledge and skills necessary to sustain progress made.

The leadership training provided a set of tools that enabled effective remote working at a time when presenteeism was the paradigm. It was the essence of change management when dealing with other senior professionals across the globe. We went from being a transactional organization to near the apex of global supply chain decision-making.

The training and embedding of the process ensured sustainability; it is self-perpetuating [see Chapter 9] and will evolve and grow over time; the toolset has stayed with me and many others for life and has provided benefits to many organizations and individuals who are not aware of its origins.

The engagement of the workforce simultaneously with the upskilling of leadership deliver employees who understand their business [see Chapter 5] and leaders who learn how to deal with this level of engagement [see Chapter 7].

Even in the complexities of a hospital with medical consultants acting semi-independently of management, Donna Roche, CEO of Mater Private Hospital in Cork, Ireland, said:

The rapid mass engagement process was a huge part in becoming profitable within three months and in doubling revenue in four years; to get consensus across the entire organization so quickly was mind-blowing and left the employees

---

* The Credo is the founding statement of Johnson & Johnson's values. To this day, it drives its policies; my mother told me that, when J&J sold her unit in the 1960s, she missed the culture so much she left. In her own words: "It just wasn't the same."

with a deep understanding of the entire hospital; the reforms made persist and when people walk into the hospital now, five years later, there is an air of courtesy and efficiency which is crucial in a healthcare setting.

The pages that follow will explain how these results have been achieved across multiple sectors and sizes of organizations. You will discover that culture change can be much more rapid than conventional wisdom indicates, and that many conventional approaches to these subjects are underpowered relative to the lofty ambitions they seek to deliver. Your organization will be able to implement RME quickly and maximize value to customers, reducing costs, delays, and frustrations while helping create a genuinely competitive but employee-owned culture.

Creating a Culture That Sustains Itself

In addressing publication bias and risks in Chapter 10, we will see how culturally ill-considered changes in senior leadership have damaged carefully cultivated cultures. My vision is to help organizations create a high-performance culture that aims to be so deeply owned by employees that it sustains itself, regardless of changes in senior leadership (see Chapters 2 and 4).

You will learn how organizations meet the yearning for higher purpose at work while simultaneously accelerating organizational high performance, and how they do this rapidly, often within weeks. You will see that they do so by creating employee "pull" or demand for an employee-owned Continuous Improvement culture and how this creates deep, values-based employee engagement and enablement with aligned behaviors, systems, metrics, and standards. They do this while continuously increasing individual, team, and system capability at all levels. Often the societal impact has been significant, including job creation and retention, opportunity for previously excluded groups, and reduction in forced emigration.

The Focus of the Book: How to Successfully Implement RME

Many books address the issues of employee engagement and culture change, leadership capability, and the body of knowledge known as Continuous Improvement separately. This book aggregates all three into a highly leveraged system maximizing multiplier effects (Figure I.1). It explains in detail how to implement RME successfully and has key lessons for any significant change in the culture of any organization.

FIGURE I.1 **The Focus of the Book**

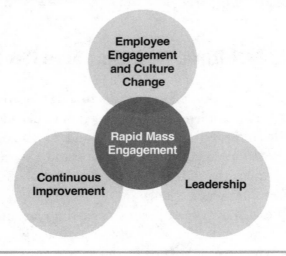

Creating systematic multiplier effects in these three focus areas is fundamental to success. The organizational results reported are the outcome of this conscious use of leverage in these usually separated fields. Employees create their own high-performance culture, and organizations sustain that new employee-owned culture via an approach to leadership development designed to embed the best of

Continuous Improvement. Cathal O'Reilly, global leader, enterprise excellence, Teleflex Inc., commenting on how DePuy Synthes won the Shingo Prize (a global award recognizing excellence in Continuous Improvement), said:

> The site transformation was built around three pillars: (1) organizational transformation, (2) process transformation, and (3) culture transformation. The Rapid Mass Engagement approach without doubt had the biggest impact on #3 and was a huge influencer on accelerating #1 and #2.

System and Leverage Effects

I will expand on the systems thinking aspects of RME in the pages to follow (see especially Chapter 5). An overview of the multiplier effects of implementing engagement, culture change, leadership, and Continuous Improvement as an integrated system is illustrated in Figure I.2.

Publication Bias

Publication bias is defined as including examples where the approach has worked well and excluding findings unhelpful to the promoters of the research. To mitigate this bias, Chapter 10 includes examples where the approach has suboptimized and explores why this happened and the lessons to be learned from that experience.

My Bias: Lesson from a 1950s Single Mother

I was born in 1954 in Monaghan in Ireland, thus ending my mother's career as a professional touring musician. She had to earn a living, so she purchased a small corner shop in Silvio Street in Belfast's Shankill ward. My mother and I were the only Catholics in

FIGURE I.2 **System and Leverage Effects**

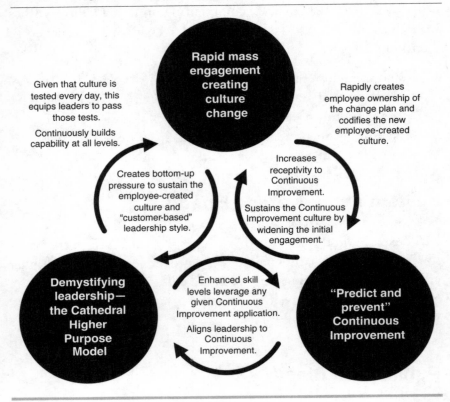

the Silvio Street area. This was generally fine, and my memories are of the wonderful kindness of our neighbors.

Attitudes hardened for some when the Official IRA started the Border Campaign in late 1956. This increasingly raised sectarian tensions in Belfast, cumulating in my mother and I having to leave Belfast under threat. Ironically, my maternal grandparents had also had to flee their Belfast home and move across the Irish border during the Belfast riots in 1920.

My mother got a job with Johnson & Johnson in Manchester, but she had a four-year-old to care for. One practical result was that she had to rush back to collect me from school before going to the shops. In the late fifties, shops typically shut at 5:30 p.m., so we often arrived just as shops were closing. On one such occasion I noticed a cleaner starting her work. I mentioned the word "cleaner," and my mother stopped to explain, "Don't see the lady as a cleaner, darling. See the lady as a lady who is doing a cleaning job at the moment. She may have other jobs also and is working to feed her children like I go to work to feed us."

That lesson is core to the values in this book. I am biased toward looking for and finding the best in others, and to seeking ways to remove barriers to individuals reaching their potential in life. This bias has inevitably influenced what case studies and ideal outcomes I have selected as important.

Serving Different Readers' Needs

It was not inevitable that this body of work would move the dial in practice; maybe it would duplicate the many other approaches that have promised much and delivered little. Both my clients and I measure the practical impact on their organizations.

At a conference in 2012, Bill Twomey presented his MSc findings about the results of my work in DePuy. I was a nervous invitee as I had not seen the research findings before this public presentation. Bill began his presentation by quoting the title of his dissertation: "A Study of the Effect of Applying Leader Standard Work to the Social Aspects of a Manufacturing System on the Performance of the System."

He then paused, pointed to me in the audience. and added: "Or, . . . is Frank talking out his arse?"

I have had more respectful introductions, but none that made me laugh more! Why was the laughter that erupted in the room important? Bill's novel opening is an example of being serious about the issues without taking ourselves too seriously. Why is this crucial? Employees and students alike express deep dissatisfaction with what they describe as boring material. My aim is to help you smile but also to learn broadly from diverse sources not confined to your sector or life experience, so that you can explore multiple innovation opportunities. Think back to your school days and of the teacher whose passion brought the subject to life; remember the effect this had on your interest and retention of learning. I aim to reproduce that effect so that you remember what you read here and are thus able to implement well.

Chapter 11 covers this key challenge in detail. It addresses the vital role of curiosity, humor, and stories in overcoming deep-seated negative and/or limiting assumptions. The latter hold individuals and their organizations back. Chapter 11 also has an additional practical benefit for the reader. I know not every story will move every reader; anytime your attention wanders, or you need a story for a presentation or workshop, or you just want to smile and be happy, I invite you to flip forward to the end of Chapter 11 for real-life stories relevant to RME* that may lighten your day and, if not, will do no harm. For readers who want an executive summary, Chapter 12 summarizes the book via Key Success Factors and provides references back to the more detailed coverage in the preceding chapters.

On first exposure to RME at conferences or public workshops, managers often express frustration that "RME is a radical culture change process, but in my current role, I lack the authority and/or budget to implement." There is so much you can do at every level: as you read, consider the RME philosophy and the practical applications that are outlined and experiment within your area. Experiment with how you recruit and promote, how you enlarge your own talent pool by maximizing cognitive and social diversity, how you manage performance and team dynamics, and how you impact your community. Indeed much of the early career development of my own thinking on these issues began with learning from *small-scale, inexpensive experiments* such as giving factory operators full control over

---

* For example, the difference between consensus and compromise is crucial in RME, and a story to illustrate the limits of compromise is included in Chapter 11.

their consumables budget and redirecting recognition effort from bureaucratic processes to highly skilled conversations between sincere individuals, both of which cost zero.

Readers' Feedback and Criticism

Success for me is you taking this book and putting it into action, deploying the insights and concepts for yourself, your organization, and the communities in which you live and work. I welcome your feedback and criticisms; the latter are often a source of the Continuous Improvement so central to the philosophy of this approach, so don't hold back! I can be reached by email at acceleratedimp@aol.com, where we can arrange a mutually beneficial discussion and I can learn from your insights and interpretation of these pages.

Let's start our journey by exploring the effectiveness of the RME approach and how it differs from much conventional practice. In Chapter 1, I lay the foundation by answering two questions frequently asked by people new to Rapid Mass Engagement.

How RME Is Different

*Everywhere I see this approach, I see systematic
and sustained engagement in improvement.*

John Bicheno
Founding director,
Lean Enterprise Research Centre

*We have seen simultaneous increases in employee
engagement scores across all regions and sectors globally.*

Peter Watkins
Global lean enterprise and
business excellence director, GKN

When I present RME to a new group, the two most frequent questions asked are "What differentiates RME from other forms of employee engagement?" and "Does it produce tangible results?" Let's address those questions.

Perhaps your organization has engaged culture change consultants, but you are finding it difficult to notice the difference. Perhaps your employee engagement scores are uncompetitive or not improving, despite intensive focus group work. Maybe you are wrestling with myriad employee complaints and grievances, or absenteeism is high or rising. Perhaps you have responded by offering perks and raising pay, but the dial is not moving. Exasperated, you ask yourself, "What more can I do?"

My vision is to help organizations create a high-performance culture so deeply owned by employees that it sustains itself regardless of changes in senior leadership. To do this, I have worked with multiple organizations to change their culture meaningfully and to increase employee engagement, productivity, and innovation. Let's examine the first key outcome of RME, discretionary effort.

Earning Discretionary Effort

To meet their stretch goals, most organizations depend upon the level of discretionary effort employees choose to give to colleagues, customers, and suppliers. The extent of that dependence will vary, but it is a rare organization where it is low. We have lots to learn from both elite sport and the military, but in one sense most organizations differ from these often-inspirational settings: in elite sport, the hurdles players need to overcome to earn professional contracts ensure that discretionary effort is almost a given; in the military, the imperatives of survival and powerful camaraderie create discretionary effort. In contrast, in most organizations many powerful factors compete for employees' finite discretionary effort. We will see how RME maximizes discretionary effort, without exploiting employees' goodwill and commitment.

What Is Rapid Mass Engagement?

Rapid Mass Engagement is a method to rapidly change culture via employee engagement, implemented with mutually reinforcing leadership and continuous improvement elements. RME has been deployed since 1998 and has evolved via a continuous process of experimentation and improvement across multiple organizational contexts.

In RME, all employees in a system diagnose the major obstacles preventing that system from achieving its Higher Purpose.* They agree on a Joint Change Plan with their senior leadership team to overcome these employee-prioritized obstacles. Agreement is reached by consensus, not by negotiation.† An employee-owned high-performance culture is also created to sustain the initial gains and to equip the system to face new challenges. Padraig Garvey, who led the Boston Scientific operational excellence team, defines employee engagement as shown in Table 1.1.

TABLE 1.1 Employee Engagement Definition and Descriptors

Definition of Engagement	The demonstration of high-performance behaviors based on the collective emotional, psychological, mental, and physical resources of employees focused toward organizational goals.
Descriptor	**Definition**
Emotionally connected	Belief in the organization, its values and higher purpose. Driven to contribute to the collective success while augmenting their own sense of self-being.
Physically involved/ Participant	Doing the work to the best of their ability and improving the work.
Participative in decision-making	Understanding of the organization's direction, with ownership and decision-making ability.
Mentally absorbed	Positive perception of the work and immersed in it.
Behaviorally directed	High-performance behaviors incorporating humility, challenge, innovation, respect, future focus, accountability, and courage.
High discretionary effort	Giving more to work in terms of time, talent, resourcefulness, thought, and effort.

Padraig Garvey, "Engaging an Organisation in Operational Excellence: A Case Study in Mass Engagement," MSc dissertation, 2015. Reproduced with kind permission of Padraig Garvey.

---

* Physical co-location is insufficient to be considered a system; meaningful interdependencies are required.
† "Consensus" here is not the consensus rightly criticized by Lencioni in which all the examples he cites are of "'compromise," a very different form of decision-making (Lencioni 2002).

Garvey's definition provides conceptual clarity for Boston Scientific's RME. More broadly, let's contrast RME with conventional approaches to employee engagement and culture change.

How Does RME Contrast with Conventional Approaches?

Firstly, RME engages, not just involves, all employees. In RME employees have power; they make meaningful decisions that impact their future; they don't just participate; they have the power to act. In the early stages of RME, employees' conversations and decisions *and management's enabling reactions* to them, combine to create an *emergent* and informal* organizational culture; this emergent culture is then codified in employees' own words, explicitly avoiding managerial language. How to transition from the emergent unsystematic culture to a systematically high-performance culture is explained in Chapter 6 and subsequent chapters.

Contrast that employee experience with the usual experience: How many times have you seen employee engagement initiatives launched with a flourish by central teams with little experience of working in a factory shop floor, warehouse, or hospital on a 12-hour night shift? What do you think is the statistical probability of employees on a physically tough night shift avidly devouring these expensively produced communications, and then having deep, meaningful debates about the meaning of words like "culture" or "values"? More frequently, employees will resent the top-down assumptions and unrealistic objectives preached at them through screens with no opportunity to contribute to or challenge these objectives. Employees will see no change in the power and influence dynamics of their work situation, precisely because there isn't any. Ruth Lawton, drew this contrast:

---

* *Emergent* is defined as "arising as a natural or logical consequence."

As Head of Employee Engagement for GKN I work with many organizations and experts specializing in employee engagement. The focus was always *top-down* engagement of employees by leaders. Employee Voice was there but leaders made the final decisions on what to do with that voice!

The Rapid Mass Engagement approach is fundamentally different in that *employees make decisions themselves* and then decide on the Joint Change Plan with their senior team; there is a power shift away from merely consulting employees to employees making decisions. This power shift differentiates RME from the conventional approaches to employee engagement.

In addition, the leadership approach is unique and global. It reaches every leader, even the cynical ones; amazingly consistent across 91 sites with so many leaders from so many different cultures, joined together by applying the same unique, simple but pragmatic approach.

The contrast between RME and conventional approaches to employee engagement and culture change is summarized in Table 1.2.

In RME employees create their new culture and Joint Change Plan (see Chapter 5); there is, therefore, no need to "sell" it to them. In this sense, management doesn't engage employees; in RME, management instead initiates a process through which employees become engaged. Leaders then work with employees to sustain the new culture that is created. Put differently: RME creates a local tiger; management feeds and sustains the tiger and ensures it bites the right things! This book shows you how to create the tiger and how to develop the leaders needed to sustain it. However, none of this can work without trust.

TABLE 1.2 **Contrast with Conventional Approaches**

Issue	Conventional Approach	RME
Method of establishing the culture	Culture is created by corporate or local senior leadership and then sold to employees.	Employees create and own their own culture.
Extent of employee power to make decisions	Employees "have a say or a voice" or are "involved" or "consulted," but the power to make the final decisions remains with management alone.	Throughout RME employees have adult-adult conversations and make decisions. They don't "ask management" or "make representations," they make decisions and actively prioritize them. They do not produce "wish lists" for managers and specialists to act on, they make and act on their own decisions with the support of those groups.
Passivity	Employees receive the culture from "on high." They are engaged *by management*.	Employees are not the passive recipients of "engagement": rather they act on their system of work in such a way that they become actively engaged. They create their own new culture and Joint Change Plan.
Cynicism, restrictive assumptions, and psychological filters	These are usually not explicitly addressed.	These are explicitly identified and addressed via the creation of curiosity, the use of humor, and targeted stories (see Chapter 11); employees are provided with proven antidotes often in the form of anecdotes and analogies that are designed to spread virally and push back against negativity. This enhances the confidence and effectiveness of employees generally, but specifically for *those employees previously intimidated by less open-minded colleagues.*

How Is Employee Trust Created in RME?

If employees are to dedicate an increased share of their discretionary effort to their work, they must first trust the RME process. When employees start their initial RME workshop (see Chapter 5), they frequently state that they do not trust the RME facilitator or their management. It is important not to be judgmental about employees' lack of trust at this stage. Indeed, I explicitly tell participants in these workshops that, given the radical nature of RME, skepticism is a sign of intelligence. Many employees share examples of their managers responding defensively to their attempts to raise issues. In contrast, in the initial RME workshops, employees begin to realize that the facilitator is genuinely trying to understand their issues. This creates curiosity and helps open previously closed minds (see Chapter 11).

The situation in each organization is unique, but after listening to over 30,000 employees in RME workshops, I found common causes of their skepticism. One was the widespread failure to integrate employee input, early enough to make a meaningful difference, into the original design and manufacture of the systems and equipment employees use. Employees also justify their distrust of management by repeating the media prominence given to business scandals, citing senior management lack of courage, integrity, and accountability. In contrast, employees are mostly unaware of examples of the opposite leadership behaviors, even when these examples are truly inspirational.*

RME creates mutually respectful, nonhierarchical, and psychologically safe but challenging conversations that cumulatively build trust. These conversations are designed to gently challenge negative and limiting assumptions and biases, including generalized biases about management's motives and capability. In RME, the key is that employees make decisions central to their future life—they don't just "have a voice." Employees notice that difference, and as RME delivers what it promises, trust grows. However, trust is fragile in nature; to prevent trust from being lost as time passes, powerful accountability is required to sustain it. Let's look at an example.

---

* To test this, check how many are aware of Tata's superb support for their employees, suppliers, and communities after the Mumbai terrorist attack outlined in Chapter 4.

Multidirectional Accountability

RME creates strong energy, drive, and mechanisms for employees to hold their leaders and themselves accountable. You will find examples threaded throughout this book; let's start with a powerful display of courage.

In one RME, I was asked to come back to train new leaders in the Cathedral Higher Purpose Model program (henceforth CHPM), the bespoke RME leadership approach outlined in Chapter 7. CHPM is designed to sustain the employee-created culture and to create highly competitive leadership capability.

In this leadership approach, there are no executive summaries for senior people; all leaders at all levels learn together using the same materials. Leaders are expected to develop their staff in these skills and in this approach. To achieve this to the required standard, they must understand every detail, and then model and reference what they have learned in their daily behavior. (How this is done is detailed in Chapter 7.) All leaders are held accountable, from above and below, to do this (see "Accountability Coaching" in Chapter 7).

This training group of over 20 leaders included both new leaders recruited externally, including a new senior leadership team member, and several frontline leaders. The latter were appointed following the removal of artificial barriers to promotion that had previously prevented progression for many shop-floor employees (see "Recruit and Promote on Traits" in Chapter 12).

The group was discussing how unique it was for employees to have created the site's local Behavioral Standards rather than have a culture imposed by management. At this point the new senior leader said to the group: "You do realize that the senior team may review and change these Behavioral Standards." The whole group looked at me for clarification.

I decided to wait to see the group's response; it was a good test of how well understood the employee-owned aspect of the culture was. The externally recruited managers found the senior leader's intervention perfectly OK—it aligned with their experience of how hierarchy and power operated where they had worked before. In contrast, those promoted from within looked very uncomfortable and looked at each other nervously.

Eventually, one leader, hands trembling, pointed to their Behavioral Standard posted on the wall that required anything that would undermine the new culture to be challenged. He said: "This culture is not yours to change." Another said: "These are our Behavioral Standards; they came from every employee's input and were created by us; they can't be unilaterally reviewed by anyone." A few more interventions followed focusing on the employee-owned aspect of the site's Behavioral Standards, and, after a tense pause, the new senior leader said, "Oh, I see. I just meant that over the years events may change and we may have to adapt." Another said, "Yes, for sure, and the key word there is 'we,' not the senior team."

The frontline leaders didn't know the character of that new senior leader. He probably did not like being challenged in public by frontline leaders three levels below him in the hierarchy. This is an example of why one of the Behavioral Standards arising from RME specifies how to sustain the culture when anyone acts against it. The challenge for all newly created cultures is: If you believe in your new culture, you must fight for it. You can't walk past when it is undermined by anyone regardless of how senior they are.

Those frontline leaders understood how damaging it would be if the story left the room that a member of the senior leadership team felt he had the right to alter what was agreed on with the workforce, a key aspect of the authenticity of RME. They took courage from their explicit Behavioral Standard to challenge any threat to their new culture, and they then modeled it by challenging the most senior person in the room in public. They took considerable career risk, and they led by example.

The senior leader had not understood the power of a workforce truly owning their own culture, nor the extent to which they were prepared to take risks to protect it. On hearing of these examples, many leaders wonder if RME could work in their organizations.

Will RME Work in My Organization?

Executives considering RME often ask: "How do we know this will work here?" No organization can know what the outcomes of RME will be, and the very lack of ability to manipulate the outcomes is key to winning the trust of employees. RME is emergent: the diagnostic process leads to laser focus on the most important issues, and then on their joint resolution. Senior management and entire workforces combine in a nonhierarchical way that changes the culture as a natural or logical result of this process. (See "The Bow Wave Effect" in Chapter 5.)

Senior leaders are frequently shocked by the power and passion of the initial RME employee feedback; sheltered behind tiers of management reporting and the unintended consequences of "management by exception" (that is, focusing on problems without sufficiently recognizing what is going well; see "Managing on Green" in Chapter 7), they have often overestimated their knowledge of the reality in their organizations. In one memorable, case a director joined the end of a night shift employee workshop (outlined in Chapter 5) to listen to the feedback. When employees provided lurid descriptions of what happened during the night shift, he went home and drank so much alcohol he was incapable of driving to work the next day! He recovered to play a leading role in implementing a highly competitive and job-creating culture on his site.

I am often asked, "We understand RME is emergent and specific outcomes cannot be guaranteed, but can overall success be guaranteed?" In response, I explain that before embarking on RME I recommend a diagnostic and decision-making event with the senior team concerned to make the go/no go decision; if the decision is to proceed, the implementation is designed to meet the bespoke needs of the specific organization; if the extent and/or speed of change is smaller, a less radical implementation is chosen. In contrast, if the joint diagnosis demonstrates that a powerful intervention is required to deliver the strategy, embracing the uncertainty of proceeding with the RME process will deliver innovation, engagement, and competitiveness.

In addition, the senior team itself must have the depth of alignment, commitment, and capability necessary to undergo the process. We can learn from the experiences of the courageous leaders who have already implemented RME (summarized in Chapter 12). As Boston Scientific's Padraig Garvey said: "The senior team had seen it work in other places, and the whole-system approach was exactly what we needed."

Just like employees, senior leaders grow to trust the process as they experience RME as *both* adaptable to the needs of the organization and uncompromising in its authenticity. Executives often ask me how the dial will move—what quantifiable outcomes will be achieved. These pages include many quantifiable outcomes that users have attributed to applying RME or its related leadership methodology, but each organization is unique. These results have happened alongside multiple other crucial inputs. These include the impact of individual leaders' integrity, courage, and energy and the previous cumulative good work of individuals in the organization.

In addition, not everything important can be measured. In an interview, Chris Thomson, site manager at Vale, addressed this measurement issue, saying:

> If you don't want to blow up your site it helps if every employee's eyes are alert to the safety issues and all feel psychologically safe to call out any risks; RME's encouragement of respectful challenge and Behavioral Standards strengthened us there and reduced the probability of disaster. How can that be quantified?

Can These Concepts Be Partially Implemented?

Jon Tudor, president of the Association for Manufacturing Excellence, works with multiple organizations at the leading edge of Continuous Improvement practice, and he noted: "I visit and assess many factories, and this is by far the most thorough and developed employee engagement strategy and execution that I have seen." The strategy is "thorough and developed," but can it also be seen as an à la carte menu? Is there value to organizations in picking and choosing from the array of processes and methods included in RME?

The first stage in RME is a senior team workshop to diagnose the levels of employee engagement and enablement they have in their organization, and what levels are needed to match the ambition of their vision and objectives. It is common for leaders' existing plans to be severely weaker than their ambitions. I advise such senior teams that "if you wish the ends, you must will the proportionate means to achieve those ends." For some senior teams, this mismatch cannot be overcome and the decision not to proceed with RME is the correct one.

Executives also ask what would happen if they chose to only implement some aspects of the full RME process. The full RME process will not be appropriate in some organizational contexts, and this has often led to innovative bespoke solutions that have driven results. An example is how Liam Keary's (now vice president global head of quality, Mallinckrodt Pharmaceuticals) quality team applied the Behavioral Standards component of RME. He said:

> I had experienced the power of the Behavioral Standards approach in both a large factory and a global supply chain organization. I realized the opportunity of applying this learning across our multiple quality locations. We reached consensus on common Behavioral Standards across all business units. We drove greater consistency of outcomes while simultaneously building more productive relationships globally. This built trust and advanced collaboration across the global virtual team avoiding conflicting priorities. All of this was achieved without any structural changes and at minimal cost.

My conclusion is that whatever the senior team agrees on at that diagnostic and decision-making workshop, the concepts, ideas, values, and practices discussed will add value. Even a decision not to proceed provides valuable clarity.

Does RME Work in Unionized Environments?

I invite you to walk in the shoes of a senior trade union representative. You have worked for years to represent employees; you understand where you work and its history; you have seen senior leaders come and go with big ideas but smaller longevity; you negotiate on behalf of employees. Your *indirect* method of management-employee relations works for you.

Then one day, this guy arrives with a very powerful form of *direct* employee-management relations. To compound this "danger" to your way of representing your members, much more wide-ranging decisions than you have ever experienced are going to be agreed on. These decisions will be made not by you and your committee but by a much larger group, representing union members and non-union members alike.

You do not have to be a conspiracy theorist to be suspicious that the union you are so proud of is about to be undermined, and it is perfectly reasonable to suspect that you are about to be disintermediated. This reasonable concern must be addressed head-on; skepticism will be sky-high; trust will be minimal and must be earned quickly and deeply. I had the advantage of being a lay union official in my early twenties, and the facilitator or facilitators you choose need to have a track record of building trust and credibility quickly in situations where relations with management can be toxic. (See "Select External Facilitators Using RME Criteria" in Chapter 12.) As an example of the atmosphere sometimes encountered, in one RME, large groups of employees refused to shake my hand as they entered their initial workshop and angrily questioned my sincerity. The lesson for senior leaders in such environments is, don't send facilitators with knives into a gunfight!

To address this understandable fear of being undermined, I designed a specific trade union workshop into RME. This union workshop addresses these issues using union frames of reference and often leads to committed and enthusiastic support from most union representatives. This has resulted in the elimination of strikes and references to third-party conflict mechanisms. Subsequently, both management and unions learn to operate in a win-win manner that provides a more productive route to overcoming differences.

A tip for the facilitation of such workshops is that understanding the goals and values of the original nineteenth-century trade union founders is valuable. This is not manipulative, or PR spin; the values of a senior leader implementing RME tend to align with the nineteenth-century goals of maximizing workforce safety, development, and opportunity. With that common ground you need only to add expert facilitation skills, stamina, and framing to enable success.

Will RME Work in My Country/ Sector/Technology?

When asked how widely applicable RME's leadership approach is, Bryan Saunders, then business development director, Middle East, Methanex, replied:

> Everywhere I have applied the Cathedral Model in BP and in Methanex—from the Far East to Africa to Europe—the fusion of recognition, coaching, and constructive feedback has always been incredibly well received.

RME has a successful track record in services as well as manufacturing, unionized and non-unionized environments, large and small locations and globally—one organization implemented the leadership and Continuous Improvement aspects of RME across 91 locations on every continent.

Common Leadership Frustrations

Once RME begins, it is not only employees who voice their frustrations; managers also contribute their diagnosis of what stops them doing a great job. Many explain how they are struggling to meet and align the yearning for higher purpose from many of the most talented and dedicated employees and are perplexed by leadership development programs that fail to increase engagement, improve results, or reduce variability. Others outline Continuous Improvement initiatives that are not achieving employee buy-in and talk of being distracted from their core role of maximizing the engagement and productivity of their teams—often by routine administrative tasks that were previously the responsibility of administrative staff. (See "Let Your Leaders Lead" in Chapter 7.) Some struggle under the non-value-adding burden of conflictual relations across functions and difficult management-employee trust issues. I will address these frustrations in Chapters 2, 7, and 12.

Sample RME Results

Does RME move the dial? John Bicheno, a leading authority on Continuous Improvement and founding director of the Lean Enterprise Research Centre, summarized the impact of RME this way: "Everywhere I see this approach, I see systematic and sustained engagement in improvement."

Anthony Collins, CEO of Topflight Group, stresses the rapid nature of results achieved even in the most difficult of circumstances: "We would not have been able to manage Brexit and Covid simultaneously, combined with another recession, without this process into profitability; I work with senior guys, but I had never before seen the 'stop, let's do it now' approach, that sense of how quickly things can happen. The sheer pace signaled urgency."

What other outcomes are reported by users of RME? In the following sections I will provide a sample of the impact across diverse sectors.

Net Promoter Scores—Customers and Employees

Two clients interviewed for this book shared their Net Promoter Scores for employees and customers. The results were an employee

NPS increase from 14 percent to 68 percent in the first year after RME for one, and for the other, customer NPS of 80 percent, four times better than leading global brands in their sector.

External Audits

James Winters, then site director, recounted that when the Shingo Institute audited DePuy Synthes's Ringaskiddy plant in 2014, they reported: "The best example we have seen of an organization that truly embraces the cultural aspects of The Toyota Way to deliver sustainable results." Richard Davies reported that when Investors in People surveyed Coca-Cola employee attitudes before and then immediately after the implementation of RME, they reported: "The greatest transformation in employee attitudes ever witnessed."

Research Findings

The research findings from two 2011 MSc dissertations into the effects of RME found tangible metric improvements in the first three years (Twomey 2011 and Whyte 2011). Productivity increased by 73 percent, absenteeism reduced by 45 percent, manufacturing lead times reduced by 76 percent, and there was a 300 percent increase in ideas implemented per employee. Significantly, Twomey found that in the one value stream where the CHPM was not implemented well (see Chapter 7), both the absenteeism and the engagement score results were much less impressive. These results were significantly impacted by a well-structured Continuous Improvement approach (see leverage effects in Figure I.2 in the Introduction).

Client Outcomes: Outokumpu, Coca-Cola, Amazon, GKN

When interviewed about the RME process in Outokumpu, Olof Faxander, the site general manager at the time, stressed the rapid nature of improvements made (hence "Rapid" in "Rapid Mass Engagement"). He also emphasized the impact on both business results and intangible but crucial improvements such as employee trust in management, saying, "The process accelerated trust quickly and had real tangible impact; HQ thought it was a reporting error when we reduced working capital by 30 percent within six months!"

Moving beyond the rapid aspect of RME stressed by Olof, Coca-Cola's Steve Adams, supply chain director (Europe), Coca-Cola European Partners, emphasized the medium-term impact on a previously underperforming site: "The performance improvements delivered over a period of three years moved one factory from significantly underperforming to becoming the Cranfield FMCG factory of the year."

Many interviewees testify about the impact of the CHPM leadership approach and of the emphasis on leveraging engagement, leadership, and Continuous Improvement. An example is Amazon Foods USA's director operations, Matt Reddick:

> I use and teach the skills and tools I learned every day—this has directly and indirectly helped an uncountable number of people. It has enabled me to scale my results across my 10 locations: my monthly development sessions with all my leaders start with considering the key diagnostic and decision-making models which are one of only two items pinned on my laptop! It is only by adding this to lean that the financial benefits are realized.

Some readers will be responsible for global lean programs, and Peter Watkins's (then global lean enterprise and business excellence director, GKN) experience is relevant here: "We have seen simultaneous increases in employee engagement scores across all regions and sectors globally."

We have heard from senior leaders, so let's hear from employee and trade union voices.

Employee Feedback

Two examples of employee feedback are typical: In 2015, a shop floor employee described how she had applied facilitation skills both at work and at home, saying, "This process has changed my life." Another common response comes from a senior trade union representative at Becton Dickinson's Consensus Day,* who noted, "I have worked here for over 20 years; before today if you had told me what we have achieved today I would have thought you were mad; this is the best day of my working life." We will examine a more detailed academic study of RME feedback in Chapter 5.

Does This Work in Practice?

At conferences and workshops, a common reaction to RME is "this sounds too good to be true; how do we know it will work?" Let's address that now.

How Coca-Cola Repeated the Lesson from Vietnam

Steve Thorpe ran several factories for Coca-Cola Enterprises in the United Kingdom. If a factory was underperforming, Steve was often summoned; his bosses knew he would turn it around, and he would turn it around through his people. In each factory, he ensured that all his leaders were trained in the RME leadership approach.

One day, a senior learning and development executive on a factory visit asked him, "Steve, why do you use this unconventional leadership training (visible in the factory) when we have such good corporate leadership material available?" Steve's reply was: "Because it always works."

In the Vietnam war, a visiting lieutenant colonel noticed his special forces carrying the Vietcong's AK-47 rather than the US standard issue M16 rifle. The lieutenant colonel asked why they were using the AK-47, a much simpler and cheaper design. He got a similar response: "Sir, because it always works" (Dockery 2009). The M16 had many strengths, but if a soldier's rifle jammed in the humidity of close-quarter jungle combat, that soldier usually died.

---

* Consensus Day is the decision-making event that agrees by consensus the management-employee Joint Change Plan within RME. This is explained in detail in Chapter 5.

The conclusion: whether you are engaged in close-quarter combat in the Vietnamese jungle or making a factory or team competitive, there is a premium on things that work and a massive opportunity cost when implementing approaches that were not designed with that overriding design criterion.

No Longer Second-Class Citizens in Rolls-Royce

In Rolls-Royce a very high percentage of employees are engineers and scientists. Sue Savage's (then general manager experimental logistics, Rolls-Royce) business was a physically disparate logistics group. They were often excluded from the many scientific and technical activities necessary to maintain the company's competitiveness, and they trended toward the bottom in engagement survey scores. Sue commented on the effect of RME on her employees: "My guys saw themselves as second-class and non-core; for them to outperform their core and much better paid and regarded colleagues in Rolls-Royce is remarkable and a massive business transformation." Employee quotes from the initial diagnostic workshops included statements such as: "We are an afterthought," "We are second-class," "They only have time for the technical people," and "If you haven't got a degree you don't matter."

In contrast, after RME, they scored 14 percent above the Rolls-Royce PLC average for teamwork and between 4 and 11 percent above average in 10 of the 14 categories in the Rolls-Royce employee survey. As one employee said: "We mattered; we made decisions; management respected our experiences and ideas. We are not second-class anymore."

"But Does It Work in Theory?"

Let's end with a light note: Garret FitzGerald led Irish Governments for long periods between 1981 and 1987. He worked tirelessly to promote understanding of the Unionist community among the population of the Republic of Ireland and an understanding of the wider Irish situation in Great Britain.* It was in the latter capacity that he traveled over to my UK university twice to speak at debates I organized on the Northern Ireland issue. He was a wonderful man, but his political opponents saw a weakness in his previous experiences as an economist or, as they saw it, "a theorist."

The story goes that FitzGerald was seeking feedback from his cabinet colleagues on the implementation of a key government policy. As he went around the cabinet table asking for each minister's feedback, minister after minister enthusiastically outlined how excellent the policy was working in practice. As more and more ministers joined this happy harmony, FitzGerald got visibly irritated before shouting: "I know it works in practice. But does it work in theory?"

This is likely untrue, but it is a good example of the power of humor, in this case deployed by political opponents, to remind the electorate of any perceived weaknesses even in the best of people. Like FitzGerald I believe there is nothing more practical than a good theory, provided it has been tested in action and modified accordingly. Having looked at why RME is different and highly practical, it is crucial to understand that it does not merely impact organizational life. In Chapter 2, we will examine how RME impacts society.

---

* Northern Ireland is part of the United Kingdom, but not part of Great Britain.

Why This Matters: The Increased Yearning for Purpose and Meaning at Work

By not understanding what their employees are running from, and what they might gravitate to, company leaders are putting their very businesses at risk.

DeSmet et al.
in *McKinsey Quarterly*, September 2021

Why does rapidly increasing employee engagement matter? What current issues that trouble the sleep of senior leaders are we offering new insights into? Let's examine these now.

As I write, survey after survey reveals employees wanting their work to provide more than just a wage or a career. Employees want their values to be reflected in their work and to have a purpose beyond organizational success.

Alongside this yearning for purpose there are opposite developments with regular reports of "crony capitalism." In this distorted form of capitalism, the true competition inherent in a well-functioning market is undermined by producer capture, insider trading, rent-seeking,* and the use of lobbying to gain unfair competitive advantage. Influential commentators have noticed this trend. Matthew Syed commented:

> Capitalism is . . . when companies compete in a free market, with some succeeding and others failing . . . (when) we see innovation and growth. Dynamism comes from the challenge of new ideas from outsiders defying the status quo, from "creative destruction." This is also what drives meritocracy, social mobility and other blessings. . . . This is what the West has squandered without realizing it.[†]

In 2019, on behalf of the editorial board of the *Financial Times*, Martin Wolfe wrote:

> What we increasingly seem to have . . . is an unstable rentier capitalism, weakened competition, feeble productivity growth, high inequality and, not coincidentally, an increasingly degraded democracy. (Wolfe 2019)

How have organizations responded to the twin developments of employee yearning for meaning at work and trends in capitalism that have alienated those employees? Historically, private-sector organizations have failed to articulate the positive societal impact of globally successful organizations on key issues such as social mobility and job creation. Engaging in this way is often seen as "political" and risky and is not a core competence for most senior leaders.

---

* Rent-seeking is when an organization increases its own wealth without creating new wealth or increasing the wealth of society. This is often via manipulating the creation of laws and regulations often to the detriment of smaller organizations, for example by creating barriers to entry.
† *Sunday Times* / News Licensing, July 4, 2021.

Well-intentioned organizational responses have often focused on corporate social responsibility (CSR) and environmental, social, and governance (ESG) initiatives while also seeking to avoid criticism by activist groups. This response has produced increased cynicism, as employees contrast the proclamation of lofty values with tangible examples of companies doing the opposite.

There is an alternative, another way for organizations to respond to employees' need to see purpose and meaning in their work. A way that provides the sought-for purpose and a way that creates consensus, not divisiveness, and ensures a realism, authenticity, cognitive diversity, and respect for differences often lacking in well-intentioned CSR and ESG initiatives.* This alternative provides a values-based and unifying narrative and avoids the unedifying spectacle of senior executives timidly retreating in the face of threats from divisive, small but vocal and politically committed activist groups.

In the current debate on purpose at work it is remarkable how rarely we look to the history of early capitalism to see what earlier generations of senior leaders achieved. The following exchange happened on a Birmingham (UK) to Dublin flight in 2017:

> ME: "Who do you work for?"
>
> MY FELLOW PASSENGER: "Kraft [Cadbury]† in Birmingham; I'm the X manager there."
>
> ME: "You must be very proud"
>
> HIM: "Of what exactly?"
>
> ME: "Of the Cadbury history, the impact of the factory on Bourneville and the surrounding area."
>
> HIM: "What impact?"

---

* Post February 24, 2022, try telling a Ukrainian defending his village against advancing tanks with a rocket launcher that investment in that rocket launcher was unethical.

† Kraft Foods acquired Cadbury in 2010, and it is now part of Mondelez International.

After a series of questions, it was clear that he had no awareness of the creation of the model village factory, of the pioneering of employee pensions, and of Cadbury's provision of employee homes with gardens and communal places to grow food, exercise, and play sports. My new flight companion had an interest in nutrition, but he was unaware of how Cadbury provided a guide to growing good food so its ex-urban employees, unused to planting crops, could maximize the nutritional quality of their families' meals. He was unaware of what his own employer, a private-sector organization with a Higher Purpose, had achieved, although he was born in the very city, Birmingham, and worked in the very factory, Bourneville, where so many lives were transformed. He landed in Dublin much prouder of his organization's history than when he had boarded.

What chance do most employees seeking purpose in their work have if, even when we have such inspiring examples, these stories are so infrequently told by schools, business leaders, and media outlets? The Cadbury family's Higher Purpose was inspired by its Quaker faith. This was also true in many early examples of ethical capitalism such as Rowntree* and Lever Brothers (precursor to Unilever) in the United Kingdom and Guinness in Ireland. In the United States, Henry Ford's motivation for "welfare capitalism" (including profit sharing and the introduction of the five-day workweek), while not explicitly spiritually motivated, had a significant ethical dimension. What can we learn from these early pioneers of ethical capitalism?

In today's workforce, the increased yearning for purpose among employees can be seen as a powerful desire to "do the right thing" at work. This in turn provides a source of energy and commitment that, provided organizations engage with authenticity, enables those organizations to meet that yearning for purpose. RME systematically amplifies that energy and commitment by uniting everyone in

---

* Seebohm Rowntree's book *Poverty: A Study of Town Life* (1901) is an excellent example of the motivation of these spiritually inspired early business owners and demonstrates how inaccurate the profit maximization theory of motivation, so common among academic economists, is. See also "The Myth of Profit Maximization" in Mackey and Sisodia 2013.

a location behind a Higher Purpose that all employees can identify with. It then provides a proven process for delivering that Higher Purpose (see Chapter 5).

Societal Impact: Creating 3,500 Jobs in a Recession

In 2008, Paul Deasy worked on the shop floor in DePuy Synthes' Ringaskiddy plant. He describes his first encounter with RME:

> We had experienced Deloitte's consultants coming in and telling us how to do lean, teaching us a lean toolbox with no attempt to ask us what we thought or what we could offer; when I heard about this mass engagement it sounded like "here we go again." I walked into that first workshop up for a fight and you disarmed me immediately. You didn't mention lean once, it was about us and what we could achieve and not just in work. When I realized this was about my kids and my community, I was 100 percent behind it.

The effect of the factory's success on the local community during the 2008–2010 recession included the creation of 700 new jobs, an increase of more than 100 percent. Applying the 1:4 job creation ratio used by a state investment agency to those extra 700 jobs, this injected the buying power of 3,500 wages into a devastated economy and its local businesses and community groups.

What prevents us scaling beyond the existing RME locations? Think of those living in previously affluent manufacturing areas that have become depopulated "rust belts" in the United States, United Kingdom, Germany, France, and much of Eastern Europe. These areas lack local opportunities, so the most highly qualified leave, creating a brain drain. Imagine the impact if we could scale the above doubling of jobs across these areas; while RME does not guarantee more jobs, it increases the likelihood parent companies will invest more in the locations that have superb delivery to customers. Many other communities could gain from this willingness to invest in locations that delight customers with their service and quality levels. This is a clear path to jobs growth and social regeneration.

DePuy Synthes is a tangible example of the societal impact of RME, implemented with passion and authenticity by a brave and talented leadership team and workforce. It demonstrates what can be achieved when employees believe that management is committed, not just to short-term goals, but also to a Higher Purpose that resonates with them.

The DePuy Synthes example is significant also because part of the success there and elsewhere was winning investment in products previously manufactured in lower-cost locations. This is a reversal of powerful global manufacturing trends. We can scale this elsewhere, to the benefit of multiple communities.

How RME Drives Social Mobility

Paul Deasy remembered his experience of RME as a shop floor employee this way:

> Without this I would have been doing repetitive work on the shop floor all my life; it gave me the self-belief to become a frontline leader and then a manager, to do a master's and to become an extreme adventure racer competing in terrain such as the Artic raising money for deprived teenagers in the spirit of this whole approach.

A key success criterion for RME is systematically identifying and removing artificial barriers that have traditionally restricted entry to leadership and professional roles (see Chapter 12). Eighty-seven percent of RME organizations interviewed for this book reported significant increases in the proportion of internal promotions from groups that previously provided relatively few candidates for these positions. You might ask what happened to the other 13 percent? They had not measured it!

Employees from all job groups became internal facilitators delivering training to everyone on their site including the senior team. This enabled these employees to use those skills—and a vigorous injection of confidence—to build careers many report they never would have imagined before RME.

Coca-Cola's Seamus Kerrigan, now plant director East Kilbride and Morpeth, Coca-Cola European Partners, addressed social mobility and widening opportunities in this way:

> The mass engagement process created numerous opportunities for people who had previously not been considered for leadership careers; we went from everyone in siloes to a wide understanding of the whole organization (three sites); this led to big increases in cross-functional teamwork and mobility; operationally, my site went from worst to best UK depot within a year.

Similarly, the founding vision of the Lean Enterprise Research Centre MSc at Cardiff University included recognizing Continuous Improvement experience and success in their criteria for selecting candidates for an always oversubscribed program. The Lean Operations MSc founder, John Bicheno, said, "We selected 25 percent plus of candidates with lean experience but without a first degree." Interestingly, 10 percent of candidates already had MBAs but recognized the value of the powerful blend of theory and practice provided by that unconventional master's program.

I am frustrated by the sheer waste of human potential caused by overly academic entry and promotion requirements. The unintended consequence is the entrenching of earlier inequalities in education systems. Clearly, widening selection criteria is crucial, but there are many immediate and practical steps that can enhance social mobility. For example, in corporate life, some of the best HR staff I selected were chosen based on their traits; they acquired their professional qualifications after appointment. This influx of individuals with shop floor experience enhanced HR policy formulation, as the voice of the customer ensured HR policies added value, rather than following fashion. This prevented idealized HR policies being imposed on situations where they are deeply unsuitable and frustrating for line managers and high-performing employees alike. I remember one frontline supervisor on secondment to my HR team looking quizzically at my corporate HR visitor and asking, "Have you ever managed on a night shift in a factory?" The proposed policy was quickly withdrawn!

The enhanced empathy works in the opposite direction also: when frontline leaders end their time in HR, they carry back an empathy for the difficulties and frustrations of the HR role. This enhances cross-functional teamwork. Frontline leaders also lose their anxiety about employment legislation and are able to deal with performance issues quickly and robustly while ensuring diagnostic quality and fairness.

Similarly, actively reversing social distancing between different graduate and nongraduate social groupings sent the right message regarding equality of opportunity. Individuals from all types of backgrounds were seen to progress based on their traits and their performance, not on their social background or on how successful they had been in traditional academic subjects. (See "Recruit and Promote on Traits" in Chapter 12.) Given this societal impact, how could RME contribute to public policy formation?

RME and Public Policy Formation

Can the lessons from RME be scaled across whole societies? Can it be scaled beyond the community level achieved already in many locations? A major incentive for writing this book is to provoke interest among politicians and those with public policy responsibilities. My goal is that many more employees, organizations, and communities benefit from what has been learned from implementing RME.

RME produces increases in engagement, enablement, inclusion, and productivity often within weeks. It enables the creation of a meaningful local Higher Purpose and a process to deliver it, owned by employees (see Chapter 5). It systematically overcomes biases and artificial restrictions limiting the career progression of employees and prospective employees, significantly increasing diversity and inclusion of previously underrepresented groups, and promotes respect and tolerance of others and their views (see Chapter 5).

From a public policy perspective, RME is not dependent upon any particular policy framework as it will amplify growth-enhancing interventions and mitigate growth-destroying ones. RME increases the probability of job retention.* In organizational settings where local high performance leads to increased investment, RME has increased jobs rapidly. Lastly, RME equips employees with the skills and techniques needed for high-quality data-driven conversations from which powerful innovation emerges (see Chapter 5). I invite feedback and discussion with readers interested in such public policy applications.

Let's move all the way from this vision of societal impact to the individual. In every organization there are many employees who yearn for purpose to their work and want to make a difference to their communities, but do not see their work as a means of doing so. They are often invisible to management until a process such as RME unleashes their commitment and energy.

"Same Body; Different Person"

A year after Bacardi's RME started, a senior leader mentioned an employee he had just promoted and said: "This process has transformed her; she is in the same body, but she is a different person." We discussed her increase in discretionary effort and the concluded that she was always the same person, but now she believed in the authenticity and purpose of what her organization was doing.

---

* For example, DePuy added 700 jobs; Boston 1,000; some RME examples avoided factory closures.

In particular, she had experienced management implementing the employee/senior leadership Joint Change Plan on time and in full. (This is the short-term impact of RME, explained in detail in Chapter 5.) She had witnessed senior leaders being trained by front-line staff in the newly created high-performance culture (one of the longer-term sustaining mechanisms to ensure the new culture can deal with new challenges). In her day-to-day work she experienced leaders modeling and referencing the new leadership standards designed to sustain the new high-performance culture. She had taken the opportunities created by the removal of artificial barriers to promotion and played a leading role in the creation of the new, multi-award-winning culture on the site. She was always the same person, but now she believed her work mattered, she had purpose, and now she was allocating more of her discretionary effort to that purposeful work she had helped create.

Helping Individuals, Not Just Organizations

I receive many emails detailing how individuals have applied the RME philosophy and skills to their private lives; they tell inspiring stories of overcoming fears, resolving family conflicts, and making a difference for others. They are my favorite emails. Bryan Saunders, who deployed the leadership aspects of RME across every continent for both BP and Methanex (see Chapter 7), said:

> This is not just for business; I have used these skills to sup-
> port individuals who needed help; the values underpinning it
> are universal and help people in their private lives also.

Societal impact matters but will not be achieved unless we understand how cultures change in practice. To be successful we need robust means of achieving our objectives. How do organizational and team cultures change? What are the key methodological issues arising from attempting to do so?

3

Designing Your Culture Change

[RME] was key to our effort to create a culture of Continuous Improvement and to look beyond just lean tools and systems.

Mike Cox
General manager UK operations, Vale

In later chapters we will explore the detailed implementation of RME and the leadership approach necessary to facilitate and sustain it. Let's take a step back and outline a top-level overview of how culture changes in practice and briefly address the design and methodology issues necessary for success.

My role in the Lean Enterprise Research Centre is to help the MSc students create what is called "Pull for Improvement" in their organizations (Devine and Bicheno 2019). My main workshop is scheduled toward the end of the two-year part-time program. By this stage students are applying their MSc learning within their own organizations. They have a good practical understanding of

Continuous Improvement philosophy and how to apply improvement tools and techniques. I open my workshop with the following thought experiment:

> Imagine if every employee at every level in your organization had complete technical mastery of every Continuous Improvement tool and technique but didn't have the desire to improve their work. How useful would that outcome be?

In RME, once employees have created the Joint Change Plan with their senior leadership team, there is a natural energy and commitment to overcome the obstacles identified (see Chapter 5); employees want to make these improvements and are hungry to learn the best methods for doing so. Creating that pull or desire is a central objective of RME. Once it exists and is sustained by the type of leadership and improvement capability specified in later chapters, outstanding results follow.

From System vs. Culture to System × Culture

Vale's Mike Cox, general manager at the award-winning Clydach Refinery, addressed the issue of moving beyond Continuous Improvement tools to creating a Continuous Improvement culture when he commented: "This [RME] was key to our effort to create a culture of Continuous Improvement and to look beyond just lean tools and systems."

My organization is called Accelerated Improvement because of a debate within the Continuous Improvement community around how to accelerate the pace of culture change. Some experts argue that to create a Continuous Improvement culture we only need the right system, because the system determines behavior within it. My LERC colleague John Seddon argues: "It is axiomatic that the system will govern behavior . . . . [W]hen you change the system your people become your asset, but do nothing to the people, for culture change is free" (Seddon 2009).

In this thinking, culture change comes as an inevitable outcome when system change is implemented well. It is certainly true that good process and system change does create a good Continuous Improvement culture. It is also true that even the most engaged employees will eventually abandon efforts to improve when faced by powerful processes and systems rewarding different behaviors. (This is the reason I will describe the need for employee enablement, not just engagement, in Chapter 5.)

The issue at hand is pace of change. The challenge to the systems-only school is the opportunity cost of running a four-cylinder engine on two cylinders, the unnecessary loss in pace of change if powerful behavioral and cultural levers are not used to leverage and accelerate systems changes. I contend that it is much quicker if Continuous Improvement is implemented in an already positive and receptive culture that creates a pull and an emotional commitment to continuously improve systems and the daily work of individuals.

Dr. Kate Bailey of Warwick University describes the experience of having a Continuous Improvement culture already in place before starting improvement:

> I have helped many organizations to implement Continuous Improvement systems and it's often difficult to create engagement and embed problem solving behaviors. The rapid mass engagement at Promed was markedly different; it created a culture where people already wanted to continuously improve their work, were committed, worked well as a team and were open to new ideas and approaches. It felt much easier to embed new ways of thinking and the improvements they made as a result were sustained.

The challenge to systems-only thinking is, why rely on systems to change culture when you can accelerate culture and system change simultaneously? I suspect the resistance to working directly on culture comes from frustration with the more conventional top-down, and Continuous Improvement–blind, approaches to culture change, rather than resistance to the bottom-up, improvement-oriented culture created by RME. RME shares the passion for engaging employees in improving their work central to approaches such as Seddon's.

It is telling that many RME successes came from clients who had stalled in their system-only improvement efforts or knew that wide and deep engagement would further increase their competitiveness. Their search for an approach that would move the dial was frustrated until they visited locations where RME had been implemented. Boston Scientific is an excellent example: already delivering best-in-class results, the senior team there conducted a comprehensive, multinational, 18-month benchmarking exercise before deciding to implement RME to further strengthen their competitive advantage.

How RME Changes System and Culture Simultaneously

Figure 3.1 visualizes how RME addresses both system and culture simultaneously. We will revisit this process throughout the RME journey, but let's consider it at high level first.

Stage 1: Design and Codify an Employee-Owned High-Performance Culture

The culture change starts with employees, rather than senior management alone, rapidly creating a new and competitive culture. At this stage, the new culture is codified as a set of Behavioral Standards representing the behavioral data prioritized by all employees in their workshops This is a key outcome of RME. The rationale and method for doing this is explained in detail in Chapter 5.

Stage 2: Minimize Variation in the Quality of Leadership

To enable and sustain the initially fragile new culture, standards of leadership outputs must be consistent (see Chapter 7). Opponents

FIGURE 3.1 Changing System and Culture Simultaneously

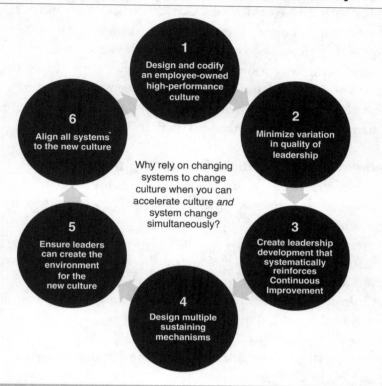

of the new culture should not have opportunity to point to examples of managers that do not model and reference the new culture; in contrast, widespread examples of behaviors such as leaders separating the situation from the person when errors occur, actively engaging employees early enough to make a difference, and challenging talking behind people's backs quickly bounce around the walkways, cafeterias, and communal spaces of the organization. To achieve this quickly, the RME leadership approach, outlined in Chapter 7, must start as soon as possible after the Joint Change Plan is agreed with the workforce. The good news is that employees invariably push for this.

Stage 3: Create Leadership Development That Systematically Reinforces Continuous Improvement

The new fragile culture needs to be sustained by process as well as behavioral change. This combination must be leveraged, and it must become mutually reinforcing, systematically designed into the way leaders are developed and trained. The conventional structural separation of learning and development from Continuous Improvement is a barrier to achieving this (see Chapter 7).

Stage 4: Design Multiple Sustaining Mechanisms

To sustain the new culture, multiple sustaining mechanisms must be designed and implemented. These include training employee facilitators, deploying them widely in improvement activities, and incorporating specific daily routines into the standard work of the organization. Many examples are outlined in subsequent chapters. These prevent natural degradation over time and aim to make the new culture independent from the energy and commitment of the original leadership group (see Chapter 9).

Stage 5: Ensure Leaders Create the Environment for the New Culture

All leaders need to create an environment where the new culture is reinforced every day. This includes ensuring that leaders are challenged without consequence.

Employees often ask, "How can we be sure our new culture will be respected if senior leaders undermine it?" This concern is why the Behavioral Standards include a mechanism for employees to challenge anything, or anyone, that endangers their culture (see Chapter 6). A notable example here is Danaher, where former executives tell of senior leaders being confirmed in their position only when their staff sign off that the new leader truly lives and breathes the Danaher Business System.*

---

* For more insight into Danaher's approach, see Koenigsaecker 2009 and Bastos and Sharman 2019.

Stage 6: Align All Systems to the New Culture

Enda Colleran, director, project management office (APAC Region) Boston Scientific, described this impetus to scan the organization for improvement when he said: "We started interrogating policies, hungry for improvement and alignment." As Enda stressed, once a new culture is created it will expose systems that are inconsistent with it, thus creating the tension and pull to improve and align these systems. We will see examples in Chapter 5 of unplanned culture changes happening earlier than pure process theory would predict. I call this the "Bow Wave Effect."

Methodology

As well as leveraging systems and culture, RME has key methodological differentiators.

Why Gorillas Don't Like Surveys: The Role of Social Anthropology

The dean of a business school joined one of my MSc workshops. I challenged the group, "Why exhaust yourself selling Continuous Improvement to employees when you can create an authentic process of employee engagement and enablement in which your employees want to make the improvements?"

The MSc students were rightly skeptical about RME, and the discussion strayed into the area of methodology. We discussed design advantages of RME, such as working with employees in real, not imagined, situations over longer periods, and with greater access than available to academic researchers. The debate included the advantages of tracking real organizational outputs such as performance, productivity, and engagement, rather than indirect indicators of performance. I stressed the financial and time constraints that limit academic researchers' access to employees. It is easier to access larger sample sizes and multisite comparisons within organizations, working with entire workforces—the M in

RME—and for longer periods than are usually available to researchers. Given the context, we discussed the "replication crisis" caused by simple statistical and other design flaws that make many studies unreliable (Ioannides 2005) and how to improve the reliability of the students' own research.

At this point, the dean and I had a short exchange on research methods, Popper's asymmetry between verification and falsification (Popper 1972), and the value of social anthropology. As this was not the primary focus of my input to the MSc, I attempted to move on, reminding the class of the famous David Attenborough film where he became part of a wild gorilla group. With a wide grin, I suggested that, lacking the vast BBC budget enjoyed by Attenborough, many researchers would have sent the gorillas a survey to complete!

The students roared with laughter, but soon after I was replaced on that MSc program. The key methodological learning points were that recording what people do and say in real situations, common in social anthropology and a design feature of RME, is more reliable than indirect methods of collecting data such as reliance on surveys, that sample size matters, and that sustaining results is crucial, so results must be tracked for long enough to detect lag effects. I also learned it is commercially unwise to entertain your students at the (perceived) expense of your client.

Learning from da Vinci: Reaggregating Learning and Merging the Science and Social Science Learning Streams

Leonardo da Vinci was a painter, but he was also an engineer, a scientist, an inventor, and an architect. Over the centuries, as total aggregate knowledge increased, knowledge became more specialized, and polymaths became rare. Let's explore the benefits of seeing knowledge in a comprehensive way by the deliberate reuniting of strands of knowledge that have become separated by specialization.

My contention is that two distinct intellectual streams have developed that are relevant to RME. These streams are typically populated by distinct professions with distinct learning backgrounds.

As an example, we can envisage what we now call coaching starting with the ancient Greeks, disappearing during the Dark Ages, and reemerging partially during the Enlightenment and later with the development of psychoanalysis in the late nineteenth century. Another driver of this intellectual stream was the challenge of how to manage the larger organizations made possible by mass production in the nineteenth century. These organizations outgrew the limited number of family members available and necessitated the introduction of professional management.

Meanwhile, as science advanced in parallel, the questions of how to create energy, what materials could be used in manufacturing, and others drove profound advances in the likes of mathematics, physics, chemistry, and metallurgy. Organizations employed specialists in these fields to deploy these advances; this was the second intellectual stream. In modern times we can see these two intellectual streams represented by their own functional specialties and populated by individuals with corresponding backgrounds as represented in Table 3.1.

TABLE 3.1 **Two Intellectual Streams**

Intellectual Stream	Coaching/OD	Diagnostics and Problem Solving
Functional representation	HR, learning and development (L&D), organizational development (OD)	Operations, quality, engineering, IT, Continuous Improvement, R&D, design
Typical academic background	Social sciences, humanities	Science, mathematics, engineering

These two streams rarely cross-pollinate. I remember my boss at Shell expressing public amazement that HQ had sent him a graduate trainee so comparatively ignorant of statistics and chemistry to work in one of Europe's largest oil refineries. He told me to forget all that "fluffy stuff" I had learned at university and set me to work analyzing data to diagnose how an overtime scam was operating. When I proudly presented my findings identifying how the scam worked and predicting an annual saving of over a million pounds a year (in 1982 prices), my boss publicly dismissed my efforts with the retort: "You are not running a Mickey Mouse Students' Union now, son; in the oil industry, we think in billions, not millions."

As I drove home, deflated, I remember logically accepting that any number must be seen in context to be meaningful (see Chilvers and Chilvers 2021), but feeling shocked by the dismissal of the one million pounds plus that we saved by ending the scam. I reflected on what I didn't know and on the statistical importance of always asking, "Is that a big number?"

Why is this experience relevant to these two intellectual streams? This was my first of many experiences of the—usually accidental—disrespect those who swim in each separate stream display toward those in the other stream.

In my case, the skills developed in winning college elections as an independent against powerful and well-funded political groupings was dismissed because I was not a chemist or a statistician. In my boss's words, what the Shell graduate recruiters had told him about me was all "Mickey Mouse stuff." His disappointment that I was not statistically skilled was entirely valid, and the assignment to understand how a sophisticated scam was operating was ideal in teaching me the importance of data analysis.*

To counter this intellectual and functional separation, the RME approach consciously merges the learning from many disciplines, but always within a context of understanding and minimizing the causes of both diagnostic and problem-solving error. In this way I aim to minimize error using both intellectual streams in combination. This is achieved by deploying the organization's statistical and Continuous Improvement capability to ensure validity and drawing on psychology and neuroscience to understand and counter

---

* Many years later, Kahneman demonstrated how many researchers and other professionals are instinctively unskilled in assessing the reliability of evidence, including their own research results (Kahneman 2011).

the most common ways in which our brains systematically bias us toward error.*

Many engineers and scientists quickly identify with my Double Diamond approach to coaching (see Chapter 7); this is not an accident. This method of coaching was designed to counter the hard science weaknesses of much conventional coaching practice via an explicit merging of the two intellectual streams. My vision is to bring these functions and intellectual streams together by reaggregating unnecessarily overspecialized knowledge (see Chapter 7), increasing cross-functional empathy and understanding, and enhancing the coaching skills of the problem-solvers and the data literacy of the coaches.

In summary, depth of understanding is best achieved by accessing learning from traditional sources like psychology, learning and development (L&D), and organizational development (OD)†—but also from STEM (science, technology, engineering, and math), from neuroscience, from social anthropology, from the arts, film, and theater, from improvement science, from the military and conflict studies, and from elite sports (see Chapter 11). By merging these contrasting intellectual streams, we can predict and prevent things going wrong by understanding and systematically countering common behaviors we know cause them to go wrong. In turn, this will maximize innovation and increase the reliability of our organizational interventions.

Let's consider the design principles that emerged from thinking in this way. I have outlined these here to help you maximize your organization's success in engaging and developing all your employees including your managers.

---

* For a broader discussion on the limits of categorical thinking, see Johansen 2020.
† Organizational development (OD) is a model of change in organizations that aligns organizational structure, corporate culture, and the realities of work to respond to the needs of any organization.

Design Criteria: How to Assess the Likely Success of Interventions and Policies

Commenting on RME's rigor, Ses Ardabili, senior supply chain manager at Bacardi, said:

> Key for me was the rigor of the whole process, an example being anonymously recording the exact words employees used in the workshops; this prevented sugarcoating of tough messages and proved to me, a junior employee at the time, that the process was authentic. This was also our introduction to Agile [Bacardi's term for its Continuous Improvement process]; this new rigorous way of thinking transformed the business and changed lives. 22 years later, I am still introducing what I learned to new locations.

Let's examine how the rigor that Ses refers to was created and can be recreated for the interventions in your organization. Many scientists and engineers are rightly skeptical about overly theoretical and unproven methods for engaging their employees and developing their leaders. No process can work without management buy-in. To be credible, I had to ensure that the tools and systems offered to managers and other employees quickly established face validity; they had to align with their experiences of work and life. How is that done? How is the likely effectiveness of your potential intervention best evaluated? Here are key design criteria.

Design for Busy People Working Under Stress Whose Jobs and Careers Depend on Success

This criterion is influenced by my entire corporate career in globally competitive sectors; in a sense, it is a bias. If you are operating in a fiercely competitive global market, you need to remember who your design is for, and to focus relentlessly on the needs of busy people working under stress, whose jobs and careers depend on success.

Many designs will work in an unpressurised, low accountability, zero- or low-competition environment, but will crash and burn when exposed to the performance levels needed to win market share from talented and well-resourced competitors. Some competitors will utilize much lower employment and regulatory costs, which means we must be even more competitive in areas such as quality, service, and innovation. If you are procuring organizational interventions, check the environment in which the provider has succeeded; check where they have been tested. Above all, don't assume that what worked well in the public sector or private monopolies or duopolies will work in a globally competitive environment.

Insist on Track Record

In designing your process, it is crucial not to lead your employees up to the top of the hill and then lead them down again; assess likely success. Regardless of the prestige of who is proposing an approach, check for a track record of working in practice. What is proposed must be based on statistically significant sample sizes and have impacted real working situations, not only exercises at public workshops or conferences where participants lack the "skin in the game" that colleagues have when working with people who influence their career.

Test Sequentially and over Long Periods

Test interventions sequentially, not in combination. If you change six things at once, how do you know what is working? It is also key to test for long periods, to avoid missing lag effects and unintended consequences. As a general rule, design permanent methods for tracking progress and continue to measure so you can respond quickly to any plateau effect or worse. Lag effects by their nature do not emerge by request or to a timeline!

Reward Sustainability, and Don't Paint Rust

Avoid rewarding superficial but glossy improvements—"painting rust." Instead, reward sustainability of both culture and skill level. Do not reward quick but insubstantial changes with rapid promotion or bonuses (see Chapter 12).

Ensure the Sustained Momentum of the Many, Not the Burnout of the Few

Create as wide a change coalition as possible, so that the percentage of the workforce positively promoting change is maximized. We will see in Chapter 5 how different aspects of RME broaden the change coalition and create informal peer-group influencers operating at every level in every function. An example is the employee facilitator group.

Create Curiosity

To maximize engagement, create curiosity by designing outputs—such as shop floor employees training directors—that challenge the usual expectation that employees have of their management (see Chapter 11). Employees simply do not think it is feasible that they can learn these skills and have such key roles in their organization without changing their job role. When it happens, it undermines limiting assumptions about what is possible, it liberates everyone from unnecessary hierarchy, and it creates intellectual open-mindedness and pathways to innovation.

"Plant Once; Reap Often"

This principle is to design interventions with multiple and wider subsequent applications to maximize return on investment. An example is deploying internal facilitators beyond their initial RME remit to enhance improvement efforts and to facilitate multiple routine activities. Another example is how the RME cross-functional coaching sustaining mechanism is designed to broaden cross-functional empathy and create leadership bench strength deeply familiar with multiple functions. As an example, within three years of using this approach to coaching, leaders develop a deep understanding of between four and six functions, other than their own, at zero additional cost—no more struggling to develop credible general managers from functional specialists!

Avoid the Happiness Myth

Happiness is clearly preferable to unhappiness, but counterintuitively, seeking happiness as a goal is dangerous. In organizational life, happiness is an outcome of deep engagement and enablement. Seeking happiness as a goal, particularly if you operate in globally competitive markets, has predictable unintended consequences, which often endanger jobs and communities. A group of full-time trade union leaders once told me that they had negotiated terms and conditions for local dockers that made them, *nominally*, the "highest-paid dockers in the world." I asked them how many ships now docked in their port, and as they fell silent, I asked them what was the point of having the highest-paid unemployed dockers in the world. After that exchange we were able to have a more realistic conversation about what was best for employees.

If we design our interventions with these design criteria, our interventions have an increased probability of success. In addition, by merging the two contrasting intellectual streams, we can maximize the reliability of our methodology, and we can do it with fun—maximizing the retention of what we learn.

Data Quality Example: Survey Data vs. RME Data

In RME, well-designed surveys are useful, especially if they include enablement as well as engagement issues. Trust is key in deciding the situations in which surveys are the best approach. When trust is low, surveys often fail to reveal the true extent of the issues, creating diagnostic underestimation of their size and nature. When trust has been established by an employee-owned process such as RME, surveys are useful for tracking progress as employees see the survey as a means of building on their process and changes. This is especially true if employees have created the survey themselves, based on their established priorities. Table 3.2 summarizes the key differences between survey data and RME data.

TABLE 3.2 **Survey Data vs. RME Data**

Issue	Survey-Based	Rapid Mass Engagement
Speed of culture change	Dependent on management response, so it is much slower than if mass engagement is achieved rapidly	Culture change happens contemporaneously (zero delay) via the bow wave effect and is driven by a much larger group, the majority being nonmanagers
Challenge to deeply held limiting assumptions and cynicism	Does not address	Explicit and pervasive design feature
Confusion between engagement and involvement	Employee issues are addressed by management—no shift in power	Employee issues are jointly addressed—a significant but controlled shift in power quickly undermines cynicism
Quality control of employee inputs	Focused on the quality of the questions and design of focus groups if used	Employees' inputs are challenged by other employees in an explicitly adult-adult setting, thus minimizing subjectivity and bias
Avoidance of groupthink	Sometimes addressed in focus group composition	Prioritized via explicit facilitation focus and by the composition of groups and subgroups
Trade union anxiety about engagement as a competitor	Does not address	Explicitly addressed (if required) via specific workshop where the issue is explored using union history, language, and philosophy

Now that we have discussed the methodology, let's begin the RME journey by examining the start-point of RME. In Chapter 4, we will address the process of creating a Higher Purpose that is local, is meaningful to employees, and provides a "North Star" or guiding focus for RME.

What Are We Engaging Our Employees About? Not Just Purpose, Higher Purpose

> *Their father and grandparents had worked here.*
> *It was our watch now; we were all custodians.*
>
> **Tony Cox**
> Site manager, Outokumpu, describing
> the Higher Purpose for his site

What did Tony Cox mean by "custodian" in the quote above? I often hear speakers advocating employee engagement and supporting their case by business results and managerial metrics. These matter, but for most employees they do not provide a compelling motivation to act. What *does* fuel that motivation, that level of discretionary effort described in Chapters 1 and 2?

Context

Tony was articulating a deep sense of "why," the challenge of purpose. He could instantly answer the question "What are we engaging our employees about?" Commentary on employee engagement often treats engagement as if it exists for its own sake; leaders often tell me, "We want to engage our employees," and I ask them to explain specifically why. Without a clear sense of why, you will lack the type of robust foundation necessary for success.

Engagement must be purposeful, in a deeper way than the purpose provided by conventional organizational goals. There must be a compelling reason for employees to want to increase their discretionary effort beyond the level necessary to meet their organization's minimum standards. Managerial purpose, which doesn't reach employees at a deeper emotional level, is not strong enough to produce the type of results achieved by RME.

Depth of Engagement and Solution Space

Depth of engagement is an important metric in RME. A guaranteed method of increasing depth of engagement is to increase the meaningfulness of the decisions employees make. All other things being equal, the greater the solution space the organization creates within which employees make decisions, the deeper the engagement will be.

RME is designed to maximize solution space. When we maximize the depth of engagement, we reach emotional levels deeper than rationality; what employees experience, what they see happening in RME, must matter enough to individuals that they are willing to go beyond the levels of discretionary effort usually associated with work. Let's consider an example; before starting their RME employee workshops, Boston Scientific in Galway consulted widely to produce their Higher Purpose, called "Winning Together" (Figure 4.1).

FIGURE 4.1 **Boston Scientific's Higher Purpose: Winning Together**

Reproduced with kind permission of Boston Scientific.

When walking around the Galway site, I often asked employees, "Which words from Winning Together do you remember the most?" The most frequent answer is: "A future for our family & friends in the West." For non-Irish readers, the reference to the West is to the part of Ireland west of the river Shannon, which suffered most badly in the depopulation of Ireland during and after the 1845–1852 Famine.

By 1861 Ireland's population had fallen to 4.4 million—a 32.3 percent decline in only 20 years. Employees in Galway knew their history, not merely as pages in their schoolbooks, but from the family stories of lost sons and daughters over the generations, forced out of Ireland by the Famine itself and the waves of emigration that followed.

They understood that what we set out to do in Galway in 2015 was to push back against this history and create jobs both at Boston Scientific and in the local supply chain. They knew this would support families staying together, reduce emigration, and keep small schools and shops open. They knew that if our effort was successful, it would create futures for their children and their communities in the West just like Winning Together had declared.

It is key for leaders to realize that it is not possible to gain that depth of commitment for a managerial objective or profit motive. Employees need a Higher Purpose that they believe in. Private organizations need profit, as it enables us to achieve great things; profit is like red blood cells in the body—we need them to live, but we don't live to produce red blood cells. Employees sense that crucial difference and respond accordingly. RME systematically transforms that vague sense into explicit conversations, and integrity is crucial. As RME evolves, trust grows through actions, not words alone (see Chapters 1 and 12).

Job creation amplifies this trust, and much like DePuy Synthes in Chapter 2, the Galway site now (2022) employs 1,000 more people than it did in 2015. The societal impact of this is obvious, but why is this important for culture change? The seemingly implausible levels of discretionary effort become possible when three interlinked things happen: when employees believe that RME is a genuine attempt to make a difference to their families and communities, when they trust that senior leaders can manage the transition to the new culture, and when they start to see things are happening quickly. (See the role of Consensus Day in Chapter 5.)

Higher Purpose Criteria

For a Higher Purpose to be effective, it must be easy to understand, written in nonmanagerial language, and meaningful to employees by resonating with their history and community. It must create a desire to make a difference, beyond personal and organization needs. In addition, it must be powerful enough to inspire individuals to "do the right thing rather than the easy thing." Finally, and crucially, it must be capable of improving significant performance metrics, so that the organization has the resources to do the right things.

The people in Boston Scientific who recalled "A future for our families & friends in the West" were prepared to do what it took to achieve that Higher Purpose. In another location, we saw employees risk their careers by publicly challenging a new senior team member (see Chapter 6) to protect that purpose. In Chapter 8 we will see other examples. The latter actions cannot be explained by the belief that people only act in their own economic self-interest (which many economists assume is what motivates employees), something else is happening. Let's look at an example where employees at a crucial point in RME sacrificed their own self-interests; where, as the saying goes, turkeys did vote for Christmas.

Example: Turkeys Can Vote for Christmas . . . If They Believe in Their Christmas

In 2000, at the Bacardi-Martini site in Southampton, previous management had tried to buy engagement by driving up wages. Predictably, the site became uncompetitive, and there was little impact on engagement. In response, a much less generous contract for new employees was introduced (a surprisingly common policy response). Over time, this produced a two-tier workforce with no relationship, and sometimes a perverse relationship, between performance and pay.

In the early RME workshops, employees argued that the pay system, usually out of scope in RME, needed to be addressed. Employees told of situations such as one employee saying to a colleague, "I see you are working Saturday and Sunday this weekend. I'll be enjoying my weekend, and I'll still earn more than you."

The Bacardi senior team trusted my assurance that establishing a joint management-employee working party* and training its members in job evaluation and pay system design would address the issue with no increase in the overall pay budget. The resultant employee/ management group did a job evaluation on every position, and then

---

* A working party is a group designed specifically to maximize the performance, especially the team-working skills, of its participants; it has distinctive features that increase the probability of success, which makes it ideal for controversial issues such as pay.

had to decide how to distribute the available pay-increase budget to address the pay anomalies.

Most employee members of the group examining the issue were at the top of their pay grade, yet, when allocating the budget, they agreed that 100 percent of pay increase budgets should go to those on the newer contracts and that that this should continue indefinitely until the pay gap was removed. They had done the calculations and knew that this would result in some higher-paid members having their pay frozen for a long time, possibly to retirement. Despite this, the vote was unanimous. Individuals voted to surrender successive pay increases because it was the right thing to do for their site and thus, for their community.

Can you imagine any management proposal to freeze individuals' pay indefinitely and transfer their pay raises to their lower-paid colleagues being enthusiastically embraced by a workforce? They voted for Christmas because they believed in this particular "Christmas," their Higher Purpose.

We have established that it is necessary for a Higher Purpose to be meaningful for employees, but is this motivation sufficient?

Purpose *Before* Profit but Not *Without* Profit

Coverage of the "Great Resignation" often quotes employees seeking "purpose before profit." In RME, the Higher Purpose necessary to focus employee engagement and culture change efforts must contribute to "moving the dial"—that is, to significant improvements in key organizational metrics such as quality, customer service, productivity, and engagement. Why is this necessary?

In globally competitive markets, unless organizations outperform highly capable competitors, they don't have the privilege of making the societal impact I describe. Lives can be transformed, but only if your organization has created the resources to implement what is required. As we discussed, we don't live for profit, but without profit we are powerless to act—we are just well-meaning idealists, raging in the storm like Shakespeare's King Lear.

Case Study

Economies of scale are key in the global spirits industry. Once markets and routes to market for brands are opened, it is possible to move multiple brands through them in a very cost-effective manner. In 2000, Bacardi-Martini faced a difficult global market situation. At a time of rapid consolidation in the sector, takeover and merger options available to its publicly quoted rivals were not available to Bacardi-Martini, because as a private company,* it could not use its shares to buy competitors. This disadvantage was compounded by the large rise in the value of their rivals' shares during the dot-com boom.† Bacardi had to address its comparative disadvantage by out-competing its now bigger rivals by other means. At its Southampton site, RME was one of the chosen means.

Bacardi communicated its Higher Purpose via a storyboard, explaining how the site was impacted by the global situation. Employees learned that Bacardi would compete on engagement, customer service, and productivity. RME was introduced as a way of creating a great place to work that drove Continuous Improvement across the site.

Did it move the dial? Internal metrics showed that the operational performance improved in every area, including a reduction in inventory (and thus cost of capital) so quick and so severe that corporate finance initially queried the accounts. On-time-in-full delivery to customers improved to global number one despite that deliberate inventory reduction. For five successive years Bacardi finished in the top ten places in the United Kingdom's "Best Companies to Work For" national engagement assessment. This was a remarkable

---

* A company whose shares do not trade on public exchanges.

† In the dot-com boom between 1995 and its peak in March 2000, the Nasdaq Composite stock market index rose 400 percent, allowing companies to use their inflated share prices to acquire competitors. During this period Guinness and Grand Metropolitan merged to form Diageo (1997), Diageo acquired IDV (1998) and, with Pernod Ricard, acquired Seagram's (2000).

achievement, given the freezing in some employees' wages and the disengaging nature of the site's technology. (High-speed manufacturing processes allowing little employee discretion generally correlate with low engagement scores.)

RME had moved the dial for employees and communities, yes, but for customers and shareholders also; Higher Purpose and profit leveraged each other in a virtuous circle. This is what RME aims to achieve. In Bacardi-Martini, the Higher Purpose was created by the senior team; are there circumstances when employee solution space can be increased further to include the power to create their own Higher Purpose?

When Employees Create Their Own Higher Purpose as the North Star for RME

In 2013 I received a call from Sean Coughlan, MD, of ICBF, a small but nationally significant genomics organization in Cork. He had witnessed the impact of RME in a large manufacturing site and wondered if RME could work in ICBF. ICBF is a services organization, not a manufacturing one, employing mostly scientists. It is a not-for-profit organization and has significant state institutional stakeholder presence on its board. Could we make RME work?

My reply was that I did not know, and that the only way to decide was to meet and diagnose both the current and the desired future state for ICBF. Sean and I were joined by Andrew Cromie, ICBF's technical director, and the outcome was that ICBF decided on the most radical and, for Sean and Andrew, the most personally risky RME option. They decided to give the power to the entire workforce to create ICBF's Higher Purpose.

It is not usual for a senior team to share the creation of the Higher Purpose with its employees. Before the decision was made, we discussed the limits of engagement and which applied to ICBF.*

---

* See Chapter 12 on when it is not appropriate to engage employees.

I will always remember Andrew and Sean saying, "Our people are from farming families, they know how crucial it is to increase rural incomes; they will create a superb Higher Purpose."

This decision is significant because this was the first time a RME process was implemented with the entire workforce making all the decisions *directly* rather than using elected representatives to agree on the Joint Change Plan with senior management. It was the first example of the direct version of RME. The direct version eliminates the distinction between depth of engagement and breadth of engagement we will address in Chapter 5.*

ICBF's Higher Purpose was agreed by every ICBF employee by consensus. This Higher Purpose provided the North Star, or point of focus, for all future decisions. The Higher Purpose ICBF's employees created is shown in Figure 4.2.

FIGURE 4.2 ICBF's Higher Purpose: Our Why & How

Reproduced with kind permission of ICBF.

---

* Suitable when the numbers of employees are small enough to reach consensus when all are gathered together in the one place at the same time.

Non-RME Examples of Higher Purpose

The concept of Higher Purpose has had inspirational impact in many contexts outside of RME. Let's look at examples from India and the United Kingdom.

Tata's Response to the Mumbai Attack

The attack on the Taj Hotel started at 9:30 p.m. on Wednesday, November 26, 2008. T. N. Shrinivas reports that within the hour the Tata Group chairman, Ratan Tata, and his senior team had assembled outside the hotel.* The hotel manager's family were staying on the sixth floor as the terrorists went room by room, killing anyone in their line of sight and pushing lighted RDX powder into the closed guest rooms to burn those inside.

In total, the terrorist group that attacked various locations in Mumbai that night had enough ammunition to kill a thousand people. The attack lasted for over 60 hours, and the hotel was not secured until November 29. This allowed the management team to enter. Ratan Tata came out and spoke to the press. He guaranteed the wages of all employees and contractors, stated that not one job would be lost, and pledged to support all Mumbai victims, not just Tata victims, of the attack. Elements of the Western press, unfamiliar with India and ignorant about Tata's history and values, responded with skepticism.

Ratan Tata's words were "We must reach out and care for every weeping eye," so Tata immediately established relief centers for all victims and their families providing medical, financial, and counseling help. As an immediate relief to the deceased Taj employees' families, Tata paid 30 months' salary and wrote off all Tata loans made available to employees to buy houses. To maintain dependents' family incomes, Tata converted the salaries that would have been paid to deceased employees into a pension fund for their family for 25 years. Tata paid the wages in full for all hotel employees and

---

* Interview with H. N. Shrinivas, March 3, 2022.

contractors who could not work during the rebuilding, and paid for the educational expenses of all deceased employees' family members until they reached the age of 25. Tata also provided six months' intensive training and a gainful job to the victims' next of kin. Tata located all victims—some had fled Mumbai and returned to the country—and assessed their needs, providing case-by-case support such as paying rent, medical help, and educational expenses, and psychiatric counseling.

H. N. Shrinivas, head of HR for Tata Hotels, worked with the senior leadership team to create the plan. As he implemented the plan, he wondered if he had exceeded his authority. He presented his list of actions and waited for the response. Ratan Tata did not ask "What will this cost?" or "Does this set a precedent?"; instead, he looked at him and asked: "Can't we do more?"

Some months later, Ratan Tata asked the leadership team, "There could be other terrorist attacks in India, besides natural calamities, where other breadwinners are killed; what can we do for them?" That question led to the establishment of a large institute designed to spring into action after terrorist attacks and natural disasters to quickly help such unfortunate families rebuild their lives.

Tata's founding values and Higher Purpose created the culture that enabled this level of support to victims and their families. This was necessary, but not sufficient; it also required compassionate leadership. The modeling of those values, exemplified by the leadership of Ratan Tata and many others (Deshpande and Raina 2011), made it happen in practice.*

Timpson's "Colleagues of Concern"

The Timpson Group is famous for employing ex-prisoners. Writing in London's *Sunday Times* in 2021, its managing director, James Timpson, addressed the fundamental issues ex-prisoners and others must overcome to get to work every day:

---

* See "A New Standard: 'Model and Reference'" in Chapter 7 for the significance of modeling and referencing in leadership.

I've learned that if colleagues don't come first, you won't achieve your financial goals. Even the very best people can have a wobble. Helping someone get back on track is far more rewarding then paying a bumper dividend, and the financial benefits are clear. People who are cared for give you their best.

Each month, I get a confidential report titled "Colleagues of Concern." The report covers 3 areas: mental health; physical health; and the most common, money problems. . . . These are major issues that can be life changing. Each colleague's issues are important and unique to them. Some choose not to engage with us, but if we're given the chance to help, it's amazing what a positive impact you can have. (Timpson 2021)

Timpson has a dedicated employee with the solution space and budget to make things happen quickly, and she intervenes with landlords and others to help employees stabilize their situations. Converting potential homelessness into a stable career at work typifies Timpson's Higher Purpose and, as James Timpson argues, makes sound commercial sense also.

Conclusion

Whether it is boosting jobs, small businesses, and communities; giving hope and meaning to ex-prisoners; or transforming rural incomes, a powerful and credible Higher Purpose creates common meaning for individuals. It provides alignment, focus, pride, and an increase in selflessness. Imagine the cumulative value of creating those outcomes in your organization and in your communities. Once we have a Higher Purpose, the next step is to understand the key planning necessary and the core sequence of interventions that rapidly change organizational culture.

Changing Culture Within Weeks: The Rapid Mass Engagement Process

The greatest transformation in employee attitudes ever witnessed.

Investors in People
Quoted by Richard Davies, VP Operations
Europe, Coca-Cola Enterprises

Let's begin to understand RME via a case study and then broaden beyond Rolls-Royce.

The Cultural and Commercial Challenges Facing Rolls-Royce

In 2005, the largest division in Rolls-Royce, Civil Aerospace, faced major commercial and cultural challenges jeopardizing the delivery of its engines to its customers. This in turn would have triggered crippling contractual, financial, and reputational penalties. I interviewed Trevor Orman, then director, operations, and Mike Moran, then HR director.

Trevor said:

> Getting it wrong would have been catastrophic for the performance of the whole of Rolls-Royce. *Conventional approaches were simply not strong enough* to deal with the business situation, we had to go outside the textbook approach. The mass engagement changed the way the business worked. We went from laggards to the top performing group which was immediately reflected in the Rolls-Royce engagement survey, and we gained a whole collection of awards for cultural transformation both internal and external. It lived with the unions afterwards, they referenced back to it, it changed the trajectory of the Civil Aerospace business. It enabled us to go to a lean way of working and this only happened because of the engagement of the workforce. Unions even supported the setup of the Singapore Test facility, which was an internal competitor for their jobs—that would never have happened before.

Mike Moran's focus was on overcoming deep and long-standing trade union resistance to the type of flexibility and productivity measures needed to compete against competitors such as GE and Pratt and Whitney. Mike explained:

> Employees voted 93 percent against 24/7 shifts in the first ballot and representatives told us, "Don't ever talk to us ever again about 24/7 contractual hours and flexible working";

within a year we had a comprehensive and groundbreaking agreement being jointly implemented and jointly trained. This would have been impossible without the rapid mass engagement process and the behavioral and leadership standards that are integral to it . . . it transformed the mutual suspicion that had held Rolls-Royce back for years.

Let's step back from a specific example and think more broadly about how cultures change in practice. What are the practical day-to-day experiences that lead to cultures being experienced as "changed"?

How Cultures Change

When I speak at conferences, I am frequently given the dreaded "immediately after lunch" slot. One such conference focused on how to change culture. The conference organizers charged high fees and provided an appropriately lavish lunch. As waistbands creaked under the pressure of that lunch and eyes drooped, I asked myself, how do I wake my listeners up?

My opening line to this "how to change culture" conference was: "Cultures don't change." I remained silent as participants reacted in surprise and looked perplexed and curious. I then explained, "Individuals change, and when enough individuals change their behavior in the same direction we notice, retrospectively, that the culture has changed." The challenge is how to make that culture change one employee at a time while simultaneously ensuring alignment across individuals, teams, and functions.

Looking back at DePuy Synthes winning the Shingo Prize in 2014, Mick McAuliffe, then a facilitator and business transformation manager, said:

> We won the Shingo Prize on the back of the new culture, there was a massive wave of initial change that just kept coming; we had a double-digit increase in productivity.

Coca-Cola, Rolls-Royce, and DePuy Synthes (Johnson & Johnson) operate in very different sectors, with very different local histories and cultures, but they achieved very similar outcomes. What does RME do to impact culture this strongly and this consistently regardless of sector? Let's revisit what RME is and then discuss how it looks and feels to participants.

RME Defined

Earlier, I defined RME as a process whereby all employees in a system* diagnose the major obstacles preventing the system from achieving its Higher Purpose, agree with their senior leadership team, by consensus not negotiation, a Joint Change Plan to overcome the employee-prioritized obstacles, and create their own high-performance culture to both sustain the initial gains and equip the system to face new challenges. In Chapter 3, we saw how RME is a six-stage approach to changing culture, illustrated in Figure 5.1.

Stages 2 through 6 of this process are covered in subsequent chapters. Here we will focus on how the employee-owned culture is created and how, simultaneously, employee engagement, enablement, and capability are maximized.

RME Initial Phases

Let's bring RME to life by explaining what happens in the crucial and "rapid" early phases of it. We can break this down into the phases illustrated in Figure 5.2.

Phase 1 of RME is the initial Diagnostic Day, when senior leaders are facilitated through a diagnostic process to decide

---

* A system involves meaningful interdependencies; mere physical colocation is not enough.

FIGURE 5.1 **Overview of the Culture Change Process**

the level of employee engagement, leadership, and Continuous Improvement capability necessary to achieve their organizational goals and the process most suited to their specific circumstances. This usually includes agreeing on the Higher Purpose.

Phase 2 is the initial All Employee Workshops covering the entire workforce and strategic contractors. The workshops are diagnostic and provide three tangible outputs decided by employees, namely the prioritized obstacles to achieving the Higher Purpose, the behavioral data from which the Behavioral Standards are derived,* and the representatives elected by their peers to attend

---

* In one RME we collected 1,399 data points; see Garvey 2015.

FIGURE 5.2 **Rapid Mass Engagement Early Phases**

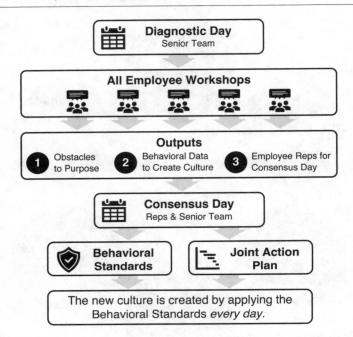

Consensus Day. The removal of the employee-prioritized obstacles subsequently provides a high degree of initial enablement and momentum and builds trust that RME is producing tangible and quick results.

Phase 3 is the Consensus Day, the decision-making event. By consensus*—not compromise or majority voting—all the representatives elected join the senior team to diagnose the current state, problem-solve how to remove the obstacles identified by the workforce in Phase 2, and elect the subteam to transform the

---

* Consensus is required as both compromise and majority voting are insufficient to build the emotional commitment to sometimes initially unpopular outcomes necessary for success.

behavioral data points agreed in Phase 2 into a set of Behavioral Standards.*

Phase 4 begins the Day after Consensus Day, when the subgroup elected at Consensus Day codifies the local high-performance culture by creating a set of Behavioral Standards from the employee data points. These Behavioral Standards are designed not only to address the immediate issues diagnosed in Phase 2, but to equip the organization to resiliently confront future and currently unknown challenges. In this way, both short-term and long-term competitiveness is addressed.

Phase 5 is the implementation of the decisions made on Consensus Day so that employees experience immediate changes and see work commencing on longer-term reforms. Sustaining mechanisms are implemented to permanently embed new ways of working and new philosophies so that the spirit of the initial breakthroughs in thinking and practice are expanded into new areas. Bespoke leadership training to sustain the new employee-created culture is crucial here (see Chapter 7). Existing policies on quality, reporting, recruitment, promotion, recognition, reward, flexibility, and so on are systematically examined and aligned to the new culture. Owners of existing policies sometimes resist this policy innovation thus suboptimizing return on investment and disappointing employees (see Chapter 10).

These rapidly cumulating phases are typical, but the details will differ to reflect the diversity of individual organizations and the decisions made at the senior team Diagnostic Day. Let's take a look at options available to sites undergoing the RME process.

---

* Why values are not sufficient and why Behavioral Standards are necessary is explained in Chapter 6.

Direct vs. Indirect Options

Figure 5.2 represents an indirect model, whereby Consensus Day comprises employees representing the workshops that elected them. In contrast, when the number of employees is small, all employees can be directly engaged without the need for initial workshops.

In all situations, employees must make decisions, and not merely be consulted or involved. This delivers deep engagement and energy in overcoming the organization's current issues. Engagement alone is not enough; if highly engaged employees crash into established systems and policies that fail to enable them to make rapid change, they will quickly become disillusioned. That is why Consensus Day must deliver both engagement and enablement, and the Joint Change Plan arising from it must be protected from vested interests attempting to manage in the old ways.*

All Employee Workshops

For most employees, the first experience of RME is the All Employee Workshops illustrated in Figure 5.2. Imagine you are such an employee. You have seen every new leadership team launch initiatives, often with major fanfare. You cannot identify many benefits from all this senior management effort. This has been frustrating for you as you experience recurring problems. You experience unequal distribution of workload, lack of accountability, and failure to deal with both overcommitment and low performance. On the morning of the first workshop your expectations are already low. You walk in and notice there are no tables or rows of seats; you see people from all departments, many of whom you don't know. As the workshop develops you realize, as Paul Deasy said, "It was about us and what we could achieve and not just in work."

---

* In one situation, the HR director attempted to retain the pre-RME policies and approaches in parallel with the new outcomes achieved on Consensus Day. This severely undermined progress.

Later, we will see how feedback from the early workshops begins to reset expectations for the workshops that follow. In those early workshops, skepticism and cynicism are understandable. But they must be addressed; the facilitator must graciously empathize with skepticism and vigorously undermine cynicism.

Consensus Day

Consensus Day is key to RME. Let's imagine how Consensus Day looks and feels to anyone walking into it. Imagine you have been elected as an employee representative or are a member of the senior team. You see people elected from every department and group sitting in a circle with the senior team. You learn that some employees worry about the manipulation of the record, so all notes are recorded publicly with no individual "interpretations" allowed. There are no tables separating people from each other. You look around and count 50 to 100 or so people in this huge circle; you know some of their views and you can't imagine how consensus is possible in such a large and diverse group. At this point, your confidence in the likely success of the event is low; if you are the most senior leader, you might think, "Why did I ever agree to be this out of control and vulnerable?"

I asked Consensus Day participants how they felt then and how they feel now. Let's start our exploration with the testimony of senior leaders. Later we will hear from employees and union leaders.

Senior Leader Perspectives

My perspective is shaped by my intent, what I designed Consensus Day to achieve. There is often a significant gap between intent and effect, so I interviewed senior end users, participants whose firsthand experience of Consensus Day would add insights and divergent thinking, valuable to anyone considering RME. Let's listen to their voices.

A key objective of RME is the total alignment of the system regardless of function or job grade. Mike Cox, Vale's plant director, described his experience as:

A day that none of us will forget. Conversations resonated with the workforce and are spoken about in the community to this day. A powerful way of ensuring not just ideas are heard but decisions are made that aligned everyone on site regardless of job.

RME's effectiveness depends on accurate diagnosis and prioritization, which requires authentic and frank nonhierarchical debate. Enda Colleran, operations manager of one of Boston Scientific's business units at that time, stressed the role of truth, frankness, and pure courage and integrity, saying, "On Consensus Day we heard hard truths from courageous people; everyone was equal, no titles, no status, no stifling of input; we learned the power of uncomfortable truth, and the Behavioral Standards agreed the next day gave us the tools to bake that into our culture."

For RME to work, negative and limiting assumptions have to be undermined and replaced with systematically open-minded attitudes toward others and their experiences; Alex Kendrick, Bacardi's logistics manager at the time, stressed the change he saw in previously negative employees: "I could see people change their attitudes in front of my eyes, given where individuals had started from, it was powerful and refreshing."

This testimony is from senior leaders in mining, medical devices, and FMCG (fast-moving consumer goods). I have detected no sectoral difference in the power and significance of Consensus Day across all the sectors where RME has been implemented. Everywhere, however, the starting skepticism is strong.

Justified Senior Skepticism

During the long and vigorous preparation for the RME process at Boston Scientific, a rightly skeptical senior leader looked at me and said:

Let me envisage this "Consensus Day": approximately 100 people elected by our employees sitting with the senior team, making key business decisions by consensus, with no

adjournments allowed for senior leaders to confer, every discussion is public. Our role is to agree the scope and then we
have no say on agenda items which are decided and prioritized by employees, not by us . . . and you are asking us to
implement in full whatever emerges!

A fair person would deduce that he was not convinced! His
reservations were reasonable and understandable. His reasonable
concerns began to ease as he learned more about the design of the
RME process and particularly as he experienced the feedback from
employees. He subsequently became an outstanding champion
of RME.

Rather than seeing skepticism as negative, it is more useful to
frame it as promoting healthy feedback and challenge, diagnostic
and planning rigor, and deeper understanding. Lack of skepticism
is a red flag on the senior team Diagnostic Day as it may signify
superficial consensus or simply following the lead of a powerfully
committed leader.* Skepticism soon morphs into commitment and
deeper engagement, precisely because of the intellectual and emotional journey required to assess the authenticity of the process,
the facilitators, and the senior leadership. Employees realize that
only senior people genuinely striving to do the right thing for their
employees and their organization are willing to expose themselves
to the uncertainty and vulnerability designed into RME.

Senior leaders have time to consider and reflect before they make
the decision to implement RME; employees first experience of it is
when they walk into their workshop. In many cases Consensus Day
is within 10 working days of that first exposure. Employees also
carry assumptions about the intentions and values of their senior
leaders into RME. Hearing from them will provide insights about
the nature of Consensus Day unobtainable from discussions confined to senior leaders.

---

* Minimizing hierarchy, influence, and fatigue are also key to arriving at high-
quality decisions in very large groups

Employee Perspectives

As an employee representative at Becton Dickinson, Derrick Dawson remembered the initial check-in at the start of Consensus Day and how attitudes changed within just one day. He said, "The first lap around the room was horrendous, the amount of pent-up anger, but by the end we had done something really good; the belief in the room came from how the issues were facilitated and it just grew and grew."

From a research perspective, Pauline Found (then Buckingham University, now Cardiff University) interviewed employee representatives from Consensus Day. Here are some employee quotes in answer to the question "Can you describe your experience of Consensus Day?"

Comments addressing how Consensus Day evolved included:

> "It was very nerve-racking at the start . . . but once it got going it settled. It became very emotional at times and there were some hard stories to listen to. . . . It was a real game changer to hear managers being so open and honest and admitting when they had got things wrong."

> "It was a very slow start, but confidence built as it got going. It was very passionate, forward looking and positive."

> "Huge level of pessimism going into the meeting and people unsure of how it would progress. . . . Momentum and excitement built as people got more and more involved in the discussion."

Comments on what was achieved included:

> "Transformative in an emotional way. Huge problems surfaced and were discussed. There was genuine honesty."

> "Wary and didn't think that people would open up, but I was very surprised how constructive it was. Very emotional at times and hard to take—restored my hope in humanity."

Perspectives on the civility of the exchanges included:

"No one cut across each other, not even in the heat. There was a lot of emotion in the room and even when it peaked this was respected."

"Quite nervous, thought it was going to be a 'them and us' battle but there was such honesty and sharing that it was a revelation."

These are a snapshot of hundreds of responses, and not everyone appreciates the time it takes to achieve genuine consensus among large groups. Employees' previous experience is overwhelmingly, at best, providing input to their managers' decisions. On Consensus Day employees made difficult and nuanced decisions themselves and commit their location to a new way of working. Power is transferred to employees who relate to their managers in an adult-adult, not a child-parent, manner (Berne, 1964); this is a key change unleashing cumulative benefits subsequently as a commercially literate workforce works with an empowering and enabling management to innovate and delight customers. An interesting outcome of this "walking in management's shoes" is how managers are perceived by employees after Consensus Day. This outcome leverages all future interactions and is an example of the "plant once; reap often" principle discussed in Chapter 3. Let's see how this develops on Consensus Day.

The Power of Humility and the Humanizing of Management

A welcome effect of the Consensus Day experience is the humanizing of management in the eyes of employees. This happens as employees experience senior leaders and other managers listening to them, building on their inputs, and disagreeing respectfully *with each other*. As individuals gracefully and humbly change their positions, understanding grows throughout Consensus Day; people begin to apologize for past mistakes and gracefully accept others' humility and admissions and work hard to secure common goals.

It is common for representatives to say, "I never realized just how complex these decisions are, I'm glad I'm not a manager!" Ironically, many do go on to become managers. This is a natural outcome as the commercial and organizational knowledge gained on Consensus Day is amplified by the consensus skills acquired on the day, and in the subsequent improvement activities. This personal development is further leveraged as employees become internal facilitators. The removal of artificial barriers to advancement provides an outlet for all these engaged and capable employees, as previously inaccessible career opportunities open up. The organization gains enlarged and culturally more diverse leadership bench strength. As Coca-Cola's Seamus Kerrigan said: "The mass engagement process created numerous opportunities for people who had previously not been considered for management to have successful leadership careers."

Wide and Deep Commercial Literacy

As a culturally significant group of peer-group respected employees—elected in the employee workshops—are exposed to information and data and make decisions that commit their organization, deeper commercial understanding grows. Imagine the effect of 16 to 24 hours of deep interaction with the experiences of frontline staff, the issues commercial staff wrestle with, how capital investment is fought for globally, and the perspectives of engineers, scientists, and other professionals of all types. I've worked with many MBA graduates who understand their business less well than Consensus Day representatives do.

Cross-Functional Empathy, Alignment, and Bench Strength

Cross-functional effectiveness also grows as Consensus Day representatives acquire greater awareness and empathy for their colleagues' issues. Representatives go back to their teams and proactively seek to prevent conflicting metrics and all the other downsides of siloed thinking. As more people better understand the organization and its myriad challenges, alignment and bench strength improves; this in turn facilitates cross-functional career moves, further increasing alignment and bench strength.

Scientific Thinking

If you believe that scientific thinking should play a greater part in decision-making, then Consensus Day is a useful means to that end. It delivers wider and deeper adoption of a scientific mindset with enhanced appreciation of, and subsequent usage of, statistical analysis, careful diagnosis, identification and systematic countering of the most common biases, and the separation of diagnosis from problem-solving. This is enhanced by the specific method of coaching deployed in the leadership approach (see Chapter 7) and by enhancing existing Continuous Improvement capability.

Duration vs. Ratio vs. the Proportion of the Workforce

There is a trade-off between the size of Consensus Day and how long it takes to reach consensus; every additional person makes consensus more difficult. Another key design issue is that the higher the proportion of employees to managers on Consensus Day, the greater the credibility of the outcomes that emerge from it: I recommend at least a 2:1 employee to manager split. Similarly, the greater the proportion of the workforce making decisions, the greater the cumulative ownership of those decisions when the inevitable challenges arise after Consensus Day.

Consensus Day Key Success Factors

The key success factors for Consensus Day are the commitment and willingness of senior leaders to be open to feedback and to admit mistakes in public, that team's alignment, and the commitment and resilience to drive for genuine *consensus and not accept compromise*.*

---

* This takes as long as it takes and requires an understanding of problem-solving techniques. The longest Consensus Day so far lasted 35 hours elapsed time and 24 hours in session.

Compromise or voting, while much quicker, would defeat the purpose of building a resilient change coalition bonded together by the experience. Given the difficulty of facilitating large diverse groups to consensus, the quality of facilitation is also crucial. We will examine external facilitator criteria in detail in Chapter 12.

How Momentum and Trust Build After Consensus Day

Momentum and trust build as employees realize that all the issues they prioritized, not just the ones some suspected management would favor, have been converted into a Joint Change Plan. That plan is communicated immediately by employees to employees, rather than via the usual management communications methods. This atypical manner and speed of communication further increases curiosity, undermines cynicism, and increases the numbers of employees willing to champion the culture change. After Consensus Day, representatives are often challenged about their change in attitudes,* and they often reply, "I was there, we changed things, I saw it happen!"

As outcomes are achieved, which had loudly been proclaimed impossible, skepticism is reduced and cynicism is undermined. The peer-group status of cynics plummets, while more quiet and reflective employees are energized as they recount RME stories and arguments in their day-to-day conversations. These more optimistic employees gain confidence, join the improvement activities arising from Consensus Day, apply for key roles such as internal facilitator, and are reinforced as their arguments are vindicated by each successful outcome. Cumulatively this moves the entire culture, gradually but steadily, in the win-win, adult-adult, Continuous Improvement direction.

---

* I have sometimes been accused of brainwashing them!

Why Does RME Separate Diagnosis from Problem-Solving?

Looking back at Figure 5.2, did you notice that the initial employee workshops are predominantly diagnostic in nature, whereas site-wide problem-solving is reserved for Consensus Day? This design is important. The initial workshops do not allow sufficient time for rigorous problem-solving. Typically, they last three hours. In addition, any tentative solutions emerging in a workshop would be owned only by a small subset of the overall workforce—the particular employees involved. Such narrow ownership of inadequately analyzed ideas often morphs into reluctance to consider other options including those agreed on during Consensus Day. The separation of diagnosis and problem-solving prevents dissipated, unaligned, and conflicting ownership from emerging.

Width and Depth of Engagement

In RME, every employee diagnoses the most important issues, everyone elects their representative for Consensus Day, everyone provides the behavioral data from which the new culture is created; no one can claim afterward: "I didn't participate, so I don't agree." In this way, engaging all employees creates the width of ownership necessary for a new culture to withstand the kind of early challenges that can undermine it before it grows strong enough to sustain itself. Depth of ownership is achieved by the more intense experience of collective, joint decision making on Consensus Day and in the subsequent improvement activities.

As the RME joint decision-making culture is applied to new issues, this drives joint management and employee co-learning. This increases and sustains both width and depth of engagement. Width and depth and Continuous Improvement capability also increases as the Joint Change Plan drives improvement projects across the organization.* The strict prioritization discipline of RME avoids overcommitment by subsuming many existing projects and challenging the significance of others.

We have now seen how RME is designed to create both width and depth of employee engagement. Many conventional approaches are not designed in this way. I am often asked to give feedback on why organizations' previous initiatives have failed to increase engagement. Let's examine those issues.

Typical Mistakes Made by Organizations Trying to Engage Their Workforce

When I receive these queries on why previous initiatives have failed, I ask what they have tried already. I find two opposite mistakes are common in these organizations.

Mistake Number 1: Naive Engagement

Naive engagement occurs when organizations argue: "No one wants to do a bad job, so if we simply get out of the way and empower them, our employees will be high performing." This logic involves two heroic assumptions, namely that merely removing leadership roles will create self-direction, and that this self-direction will create high-performing teams.

Both assumptions are dubious; the only guaranteed outcome of a power vacuum is that someone will fill it. If what fills the power vacuum is random, the results will be equally random and sometimes will be catastrophic. While implementing self-directed work teams globally at CarnaudMetalbox,† we found that successes heavily correlated with self-directed teams being thoroughly trained, including knowing exactly what was expected from them to align with other

---

* This is one of many examples of how engagement and Continuous Improvement mutually leverage each other as depicted in Figure I.2 in the Introduction.

† In CarnaudMetalbox, self-directed work teams were called autonomous manufacturing teams.

teams and the wider organization.* A simple guide is that while sharing power does facilitate engagement, merely removing management power in the absence of other powerful interventions, such as RME, does not; indeed, there are cases where it has facilitated bullying, systematic restriction of output, and abuse of vulnerable employees.

Mistake Number 2: Timid Engagement

This mistake happens when organizations aim for high levels of engagement but do not create sufficiently meaningful changes to employees' work experience to achieve it. If you wish the ends of high levels of engagement and transformational results, you must also mandate the means, that is, you must create a delivery methodology powerful enough to deliver those outcomes. The solution space available for employee decisions must be wide enough to inspire meaningful changes in employees' day-to-day work experience (see Chapter 12).

The level of engagement delivered by RME is not possible if organizations have restrictive assumptions about what is possible and are unwilling to take calculated risks. As a guide, unless employees come home and say excitedly, "You would never believe what happened today," your design is unlikely to be radical enough to deliver a high-performance and continuously improving culture. With that key criterion in mind, let's examine how RME frames the key issue of motivation.

Motivation Toward, Not Just Motivation Away From

Many argue that to have the urgency needed to drive significant change it is necessary to have or to create a "burning platform" or

---

* Policy deployment, or hoshin kanri, is crucial here. See Imai 1986, Dennis 2006, Bastos and Sharman 2019.

urgent threat to, for example, jobs. The challenge for approaches that rely only on burning platform narratives is, what happens as the fear of negative consequences reduces? Clearly a burning platform focusses minds in the short term, but if we can create a situation where employees are motivated toward a Higher Purpose, then such a motivation will be more meaningful and sustain better and longer than motivation by fear. In addition, when the threat does not materialize, the effect of a burning platform diminishes, leading to employees becoming increasingly distrustful of being manipulated. This undermines integrity. Integrity is maximized if we understand and utilize the difference between the type of engagement discussed here and superficially similar concepts such as "involvement" and "consultation."

Engagement Not Involvement

How RME is differentiated from typical involvement or consultation processes is summarized in Table 5.1.

To summarize, conventional approaches try to sell management's initiatives or culture to their employees; in RME, employees create and own their own culture. Traditionally, employees "have a say" or are involved or consulted, but the power to make the final decisions remains with management alone.

Throughout RME, employees have challenging adult-adult conversations and make decisions. They don't passively "ask management" or merely provide input to decisions; they actively prioritize, they are never in a child-parent relationship. As a result, employees are not the passive recipients of "engagement"; rather, they act on their system of work in such a way that they become actively engaged. In this sense, management doesn't engage employees; management creates a process, RME, whereby employees become engaged and then works to sustain the new culture. Let's contrast the conventional top-down mindset with this bottom-up approach.

TABLE 5.1 **Engagement vs. Involvement**

Issue	Involvement or Consultation	Rapid, Mass Engagement
Role of employees	To provide input (often child-parent) or sometimes to meet regulatory/ legislative requirements	To make decisions and joint decisions—always adult-adult
Decision-making	Employee feedback or "voice" provides a mere input to the decision-making process; employees are forced to wait for management responses and experience random and partial outcomes; this frustrates well-motivated employees who have contributed their ideas and diagnosis.	Employees make three key decisions in their initial workshops: namely to prioritize issues and create the agenda for Consensus Day, what behavioral data should be codified in the new Behavioral Standards, and who to elect to attend Consensus Day. A *Joint Change Plan* is created at Consensus Day where employee solution space is *maximized by design*.
How quickly are decisions made?	Often slowly, employees frequently answer "never"!	Implementation begins within 48 hours of Consensus Day.
Who decides the agenda? (Within the given strategy and Higher Purpose)	Leadership	Employees via the diagnostic and prioritization power given to them in the diagnostic workshops
Cynicism, restrictive assumptions, and psychological filters	Usually not addressed	Explicitly identified and addressed via humor, targeted stories and the creation of curiosity (see Chapter 11); these provide employees with antidotes to negativity that are designed to spread virally

Culture Change Options: Top-Down or Bottom-Up

Many attempts to create a high-performance culture produce disappointing results. Leadership typically codifies the new culture and subsequently sells it to employees. This is quick in design, but slow, and often unsuccessful, in implementation. How often have you witnessed the repeated relaunch of corporate values with similarly frustrating results, including employee disillusionment with "shiny and new" initiatives and the very concept of "culture"?

In contrast, RME depends upon employee ownership; any attempt at manipulation of outcomes will destroy the integrity on which it is based. What delivers a high-performance culture is not manipulation of outcomes but integrity, rigorous scope,* leaders with the right values and traits, comprehensive design, facilitation excellence, and leadership and Continuous Improvement capability at all levels—all of which are enhanced by the RME process itself.

A comparison of top-down and bottom-up culture change options is shown in Table 5.2.

TABLE 5.2 **Top-Down vs. Bottom-Up Culture Change**

Issue	Top-Down	Bottom-Up*
Pace	Usually slow	Can create rapid employee ownership—often within days in small organizations using direct versions of the approach
Negative and limiting assumptions and filters	Negative assumptions "attack" the top-down messages and training	Assumptions and filters are systematically undermined by achieving outcomes seen as "impossible" to the skeptical and cynical; this creates employee curiosity
Accountability of leaders	Difficult due to the ability to interpret corporate values with a "political" bias (in the pejorative sense) and the small number of people holding leaders accountable from above	Strong because: 1. Leaders are held accountable both from below and above. 2. Behavioral Standards are much harder to interpret politically, making them more resilient against "political" behavior.
Applicability	Suitable when uncertainty prevents long-term planning or when change in senior leadership is expected	Ideal when: 1. Competitive advantage is sought or needs to increase. 2. Survival demands rapid and radical change.

* See "Understand the Limits of Engagement" in Chapter 12

Why "Rapid" and Why "Mass"?

The bottom-up nature of RME is clear, but why is it "rapid" and "mass"? Why so much pace? Why engage the entire local workforce rather than a section of it such as when using a pilot approach?*

Rapid

Shane Maher, senior director plan, joint reconstruction & power tools, DePuy Synthes Companies, stressed the speed of momentum and trust building, saying, "It is hard to turn the raw emotion of employee experiences into a data driven process, but that is what happened; it was scary and invigorating to move through the process creating momentum and building trust so quickly." In the initial RME workshops employees frequently express frustration at the pace of management response to their inputs. I ask employees how long they wait for an answer after suggesting an idea or other input, and I often get answers like "months" or even "never."

Imagine the contrast and symbolism when employees themselves identify the major issues and start to resolve them, within two working weeks (DePuy for 650 employees) or within six working weeks (Boston Scientific for 3,000+ employees). Imagine the effect when this is done in the same week as was done in ICBF, Promed, and other smaller organizations. Engagement must be meaningful, and the speed with which action is taken sends important messages around integrity and seriousness of intent (see Chapter 8). The strength of these messages is amplified when it demonstrates a powerful contrast to employees' normal experience and previous perception of what is possible.

---

* A pilot approach is a small-scale implementation often used to demonstrate proof of concept.

Mass

The fourteenth of Deming's famous 14 Points (Deming 1982) is "Put everyone in the company to work to accomplish the transformation. The transformation is everybody's job."

"Mass" means engaging *all* employees, not just a subset of them. Using a pilot to test if an approach works often creates a "not invented here" attitude among those not involved. This fatal lack of ownership is followed by rejection of the "foreign body" by those not in the pilot area. Furthermore, once the pilot design is expanded it is very difficult for senior leaders and support functions to give the same emotional and other support to the nonpilot processes and locations. For these reasons, pilot approaches frequently disappoint despite the encouraging results achieved by the pilot itself.

The Bow Wave Effect

The *rapid* and *mass* nature of RME has other effects on the culture change as well. For instance, the "bow wave effect" refers to how the culture changes in advance of the explicit processes designed to change it.

Alan Dodrill, people lead, J. Murphy and Sons, experienced it this way:

> The culture changed for us in my workshop before we even got to Consensus Day. Being from HR I knew many individuals in the room and their back story, I knew how unengaged and even actively disengaged some were; I could not believe how quickly they became engrossed with the prospect of creating their own way of working. People sat forward in their chairs as you framed the process and explained the opportunity for employees to create their own future. After the workshop people stopped me in the corridors anxious to know how the other workshops were going.

An interesting example of the bow wave effect even impacted those not involved in the initial workshops—canteen staff. To understand why they were not involved we need to think about the RME start point, the senior team Diagnostic Day. On that day the senior team decides the boundaries of the system we are trying to optimize. Crucial is the real interdependency among the employees involved. Interdependency generates the meaningful exchanges on issues that materially impact employees' working lives. Without this interdependency and thus relevance, why would employees engage at a deep enough level to drive a relentless high-standards and high-performance culture? For an employee to spend three hours diagnosing irrelevant issues is the opposite of engagement!

The senior team Diagnostic Day includes a decision on whether to include contractors, and if so, which ones. In Boston Scientific the decision was that canteen staff would not be included in RME so canteen staff had not attended the employee workshops.

My co-facilitator and I were having a short break between workshops. We had completed fewer than 20 of the eventual 90 workshops at that stage. The canteen manager, an inspirational lady named Aileen Mangan, group services manager with Compass, approached and said, "Excuse me Frank, my staff have asked me to speak to you about what you are doing."

My heart sank. As a man of a certain age, I am conscious that my lighthearted manner is not to everyone's taste. Had I said something "inappropriate"?

Aileen continued: "My staff have noticed that since the workshops started, people are treating them better at the tills. They want you to keep doing whatever you are doing in there!" We all burst into laughter, I gave a thumbs-up to the canteen staff on the nearby tills, and I asked what specific behavioral changes they had noticed. It was simple but profoundly important behaviors, such as a higher percentage of people ending mobile calls before going through the till, not talking across them to others, smiling and showing interest in them.

As we saw earlier, the initial All Employee Workshops are explicitly diagnostic, yet the facilitation of the workshops has deliberately implicit cultural effects. It sensitizes participants to think about how they behave toward each other, and this was what the canteen staff had noticed. These implicit effects are designed into the process at all stages and have a cumulative impact on the culture; they are one reason why the facilitator managing RME is so important for success (see Chapter 12).

Another example of the bow wave effect was informal changes to the 360-degree feedback process. Individual leaders learned the "within four eyes"* approach to constructive feedback (see Chapter 7) and began giving feedback to individuals before completing the corporate electronic 360-degree inputs. This changed the quality of individuals' experiences from receiving anonymous and out-of-context comments to individuals openly exploring the issues and working together to overcome them. This in turn increased the effectiveness of the formal review process.

Similarly, informal changes to formal progress reviews led to more focus on what had been done well, including appreciating preventative interventions (see "Managing on Green" in Chapter 7). This reinforced the "predict and prevent" approach to Continuous Improvement (see Figure I.2 in the Introduction), created a more developmental rather than blame-oriented review experience for employees, and increased the transparency of issues and thus improved quality. In addition, this cultural change to the key process of reviewing performance, boosted innovation, increased the spontaneity and quality of recognition, and facilitated the quicker and wider deployment of best practices. This is a powerful example of the "sow once; reap often" design criteria, which is key to RME.

---

* "Within four eyes" is a German saying meaning "discuss with me one-on-one, not about me when I'm not there."

Despite these multiple early wins, it is time for caution: creating high levels of employee engagement is necessary to change culture but not sufficient to sustain those initial gains.

Engagement Alone Is Not Enough: The Need for Enablement, Continuous Improvement, and Leadership Capability

Let's consider what is needed to sustain a change in culture, starting with the need for employee enablement in addition to engagement.

Employee Enablement

If the obstacles to achieving the Higher Purpose are not removed in such a way that employees are enabled to implement the changes needed, the initially engaged employees will become disengaged. Highly engaged employees' efforts to improve are often frustrated by restrictive, disempowering policies and processes often implemented with good intent but designed in a risk-adverse manner. Summarizing, your engagement approach has a twin called enablement without which it will be lonely and produce suboptimal results.

Let's imagine we have added enablement to our engagement: will the new culture be sustained? Possibly, but the probability of sustaining the new culture is enhanced if two other processes are leveraged. The crucial interrelationships are between engagement and enablement, Continuous Improvement, and leadership development (see Brophy 2012 and Chapter 7). As we saw earlier, the leverage created by these three areas of focus is an accelerant to the long-term success of any high-performance and continuously improving culture. Figure 5.3 gives an overview of the leverage achieved.

FIGURE 5.3 **The Leverage Effects of Engagement × Enablement ×**
Leadership × Continuous Improvement

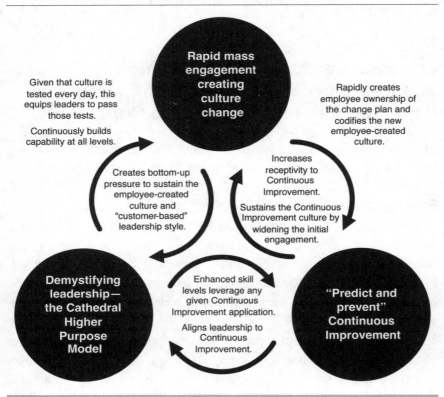

Continuous Improvement Capability

Let's examine how Continuous Improvement and leadership capability can provide that accelerant to your culture change. Cardinal Health's Paul O'Driscoll, VP manufacturing Europe & Asia, commented on the leverage possible in this way:

> The most important learning I ever experienced. 8 years later, it is part of my leadership, engagement, and OP Ex DNA. Because the models were simple and connected, the

organization gained a common, calibrated view of Standards and Behavioral Expectations—this was far superior to other discrete leadership initiatives.

How is what Paul calls "Op Ex DNA" created in RME? Once Consensus Day has agreed the Joint Change Plan to address the prioritized obstacles, detailed implementation work starts. This includes the collection of data and checking any assumptions or other inputs that contributed to decisions made on Consensus Day. This rapidly increases the percentage of employees who are deeply engaged, beyond the participants who made the decisions on Consensus Day.

To maximize the effectiveness of the implementation of complex organizational changes requires the expertise of highly capable Continuous Improvement practitioners. Well-meaning but misguided or unskilled attempts to implement the Continuous Improvement of the daily work of employees will undermine the progress made and damage credibility. Typical mistakes include failing to align with the organization's strategy and objectives, implementing suboptimum improvements, improving processes that should be eliminated, and wasting time on symptoms due to failure to identify root causes.

If an organization or site does not already have a credible Continuous Improvement capability, one needs to be created. Maximizing internal capability via knowledge and know-how transfer to the workforce is key, so the organization becomes more and more independent of external consultants for all but the most complex issues.

Leadership Capability

Many leaders understandably struggle to adjust to the style of leadership and associated skill level required to model a high-performance culture. Sustaining that new culture in the face of operational challenges when it is still new and fragile is an important priority for leaders at all levels. Working in a highly enabled and highly empowered culture is challenging and requires specific knowledge and skills (detailed in Chapter 7). Failure to provide these sets leaders up for failure and can quickly undermine the new culture.

Having explained the importance of leveraging engagement, enablement, Continuous Improvement, and leadership, let's take a systems thinking* perspective to the objectives of RME. Specifically let's explore how to maximize both the human/social and the technical aspects of any system you are trying to optimize.

Ensuring Sociotechnical Optimization

Throughout RME, including during the leadership development and Continuous Improvement aspects, the aim is to optimize the whole system—that is, both the social and the technical aspects of that system (see Trist 1981). This is much wider than ergonomics and involves issues such as the effect of changes on employees' social standing, self-image, and related issues that are often neglected even when employees are deeply involved in improvement events.

How crucial this is was seen in a high-technology client where the employee workshops uncovered widespread unintentional alienation of operators by engineers. When explored on Consensus Day, we discovered that this had been exacerbated by advances in technology enabling engineers to make systems changes remotely, literally taking over control of equipment that operators were working on with no notice or consideration of optimum timing. This technological edge had many technical and efficiency advantages, so it could not be sacrificed. In response to the accidental alienation of operators, Consensus Day decided to create systematic mutually respectful interactions between operators and engineers. These structured conversations deployed the skills and techniques learned in the leadership and facilitation training. The technological and efficiency advantages of remote access were thus augmented

---

* For a more detailed coverage of systems thinking in the context of RME see Garvey 2015.

by enhancing the learning *and mutual respect* of both operators and engineers. The engineers had been shocked to hear how their well-meaning technical interventions had impacted their shop floor colleagues, and the operators understood that their own reactions to this demonstrated the need for, and the practicality of, their new "assume positive intent" Behavioral Standard. This is an example of how the various parts of the RME system (systems thinking, Consensus Day, leadership and facilitation skills, and Behavioral Standards) mutually reinforce and leverage each other.

To demonstrate the impact of failing to optimize both the technical and social aspects of a system, let's examine an example of a systems thinking analysis derived from employee evidence in the early stages of an RME. The analysis found an implicit managerial assumption of infinite capacity applied to high performers, short-term thinking, and repeated firefighting of the same issues with no time for root cause fixes—but time for fixing the same things again and again! This prevented Continuous Improvement and innovation despite the high-quality technical processes in place to do so. It also demoralized those employees who were most keen to make improvements. Furthermore, high performers were overcommitted and overworked, as low performers contributed much less. This work imbalance had not been addressed and destabilized team dynamics.

A perverse outcome was that technically excellent Continuous Improvement data gathering tools were seen by employees as repressive rather than as signals to help employees do their work. Furthermore, Continuous Improvement was seen as done *to* operators by engineers. As a result, employee resistance frustrated the higher-performing operators and created systematic loss of potential improvement opportunities. The accumulation of this was a high but invisible cost paid by the organization due to its failure to optimize the technical and social aspects of its systems of work. These issues were addressed quickly as the leadership aspect of RME took effect.

Now that we understand how the initial stages of RME operate, let's explore why relying solely on a values-based approach to deliver behavioral change is not powerful enough to deliver the type of outcomes associated with RME. This is crucial because nearly all culture change efforts rightly place great emphasis on values. We will discover why this emphasis is necessary but not sufficient and why we need locally created and owned Behavioral Standards in the next chapter.

Ownership and Accountability: Why Values Alone Are Insufficient

*It was not a management initiative; it was how
we lived our lives . . . the process created the
psychological safety to speak up, . . . our Behavioral
Standards trumped hierarchy and negativity.*

Paul Deasy
Then a shop floor employee at DePuy Synthes
(Johnson & Johnson)

Elsewhere we discuss the significance of end-user feedback, so let's listen to other end users of Behavioral Standards before exploring how they differ from values-based approaches.

User Feedback on Behavioral Standards

We will define Behavioral Standards later, but to gain insights into how they work in practice, let's hear again from end users. In discussing Rolls-Royce's Behavioral Standards, Trevor Orman, director, operations, noted that "it was employees' language—not googled or copied from elsewhere, not management going off on a workshop and launching management words."

Employees are used to statements of organizational values being divorced from their experiences, in contrast and from a shop floor perspective, Paul Deasy, then a shop floor operator in DePuy (now learning and capabilities lead at Janssen BIO), emphasized the transformational impact on the culture at DePuy Synthes:

> When we used our Behavioral Standard to challenge people talking about someone behind their back, people noticed the difference this made, and the culture grew and grew. On the shop floor and in meetings with management, we said we had to live our Behavioral Standards, they are ours. It was not a management initiative; it was how we lived our lives. Looking back, the process created the psychological safety to speak up, to be human, and have a discussion with anyone at any level always knowing you had the Behavioral Standards as your backup; our Behavioral Standards trumped hierarchy and negativity.

Creating top-down sets of organizational values is easy, but cultures only change if day-to-day activities are experienced to be different. Padraig Garvey, production unit manager at Boston Scientific, emphasized the effect on day-to-day conversations and organizational performance:

> Our Behavioral Standards have become a passport to quality conversations, they have flattened our organization hierarchically and allowed respectful challenge in every direction; we have added 1,000 jobs while simultaneously enriching our culture.

Ownership is key to culture change, and employees have corporate values given to them from on high. In contrast, Vale's site manager Chris Thompson stressed the need for employees to own their culture rather than have it imposed hierarchically. He said:

> The senior management at our Works had previously developed a set of behaviors that we had shared with the workforce alongside the Values that had been developed by our parent company. The problem with this approach is that it is instructive and hierarchical, i.e., these are the values and behaviors that you must adopt because we say so. The key difference with the Behavioral Standards approach is the latter is inclusive and nonhierarchical.

In these examples we can see how Behavioral Standards have helped move the dial in ways rarely seen when relying on values alone. Let's define what Behavioral Standards are.

What Are Behavioral Standards?

What are these Behavioral Standards? I define Behavioral Standards as locally agreed explicit behaviors, created by the employees in a particular location from every employee's behavioral input and designed to culturally enable and move toward a Higher Purpose meaningful to those employees. Given this definition, they are written in the day-to-day language of the employees who create them, and they are owned and sustained by example and by a respectful but powerful mechanism to challenge any undermining of the employee-created culture. Behavioral Standards are the specific outcome of the local process that created them, so they cannot be simply copied and applied to other locations or groups of employees

Garvey (2015) created a set of criteria in his MSc Dissertation, shown in Table 6.1.

TABLE 6.1 Garvey's Criteria for Effective Behavioral Standards

Criteria	Description
Measurable and binary	The Behavioral Standards must be clear, unambiguous, and be seen by all
Be of the people	As the workshops develop the data in which the standards are built, there is ownership by all in the standards
Adaptive to local culture and customs	While they drive high performance, the Behavioral Standards must reflect the individual culture of the organization and take into consideration the cultural nuances of the location
Self-reinforcing	Ensuring sustainability by having a mechanism built into the standards to reinforce the behaviors

Reproduced with kind permission of P. Garvey.

Why Were Behavioral Standards Invented?

I am an enthusiastic champion of aligning organizations at the values level. I spent many frustrating years in corporate life trying to hold senior leaders accountable to corporate values. Senior leaders are intelligent and articulate and have little difficulty superficially aligning corporate values with their habitual behaviors. When this happens, employees become disillusioned with the values themselves and with leaders who, as employees see it, are playing word games rather than sincerely adjusting their behaviors to the values.

How did well-intentioned organizational values have the unintended consequence of enabling verbally dexterous, bright, and articulate people to avoid accountability? A cause was what I call "wiggle room" or the Humpty Dumpty approach to language summarized by Lewis Carroll (1865) as: "When I use a word . . . it means just what I choose it to mean."

We needed something more behaviorally specific that reduced wiggle room and made it clear when the culture was being reinforced and when it was being undermined. I called these Behavioral Standards to differentiate them from principles that, in the English language, can be interpreted as merely desirable. We needed a method to signal that these behaviors were strategic imperatives for success and thus not merely "nice to have."

How Do Employees Create Their Behavioral Standards?

The subgroup elected by Consensus Day transforms the behavioral data recorded in every employee workshop into a small number of Behavioral Standards (see Figure 5.2 in Chapter 5). That subgroup is trained in how to accurately compress the sometimes thousands of employee data points into a small number of Behavioral Standards without diluting the employees' words. The subgroup learns to detect and avoid any words or phrases that allow individuals to avoid accountability.

How Do Behavioral Standards Differ from Values?

How Behavioral Standards differ from a values-based approach is summarized in Table 6.2.

Case Study: "Whose Neck to Grab?"

In the medical devices sector, quality issues endanger patients. This creates a powerful determination to protect the patient by having a zero-tolerance attitude to defects. In one RME, employee workshop after employee workshop selected management's response to quality issues as a key obstacle to achieving the site's Higher Purpose. The response to quality issues was to immediately remove the employee from the production line pending investigation. If the investigation found that the employee was not the cause of the quality problem, then the employee was reinstated. Employees and managers

TABLE 6.2 **How Behavioral Standards and Values-Based Approaches Differ**

Issue	Values-Based	Behavioral Standards–Based
Ownership	Top-down	Explicitly created by employees to reflect the collective behavioral data prioritized by every employee in the workshops
Accountability	Very difficult due to interpretation issues	Accountability is a design criterion that the subgroup aims to maximize
Measurability	Very difficult and prone to interpretation	"Measurable or binary" is a design criterion that the subgroup aims to maximize
Identifying and addressing "what must be stopped" in the current culture	Focus is on the positive so unpalatable issues are often unhelpfully framed as "negative" or are insufficiently robustly addressed	Explicitly addresses these unpalatable issues by the design and content of the All Employee Workshops
Tendency to non-value-added discussions?	Accidentally encouraged due to interpretation issues above	Minimizes this waste by design via the "measurable or binary" criterion necessary to count as a Behavioral Standard

described the approach to accountability as "whose neck to grab?" and the shame of being publicly found "guilty before trial" had unintended but predictable consequences such as concealment and unwillingness to flag issues early. The effect on engagement and on quality issues was severe and led to the issue being prioritized by the employee workshops.

Let's zoom out from this case study to consider how conventional values-based approaches address these accountability and quality issues. Values statements such as "We have a no-blame culture" are very common. Seeking a culture where mistakes are tolerated provided learning is achieved and repetitions are avoided is a noble goal. I had countless conversations on this accountability/blame issue where articulate leaders responded to my feedback by saying, "But Frank, that wasn't blame; it was accountability."

One of the criteria for determining whether a statement is a Behavioral Standard rather than a mere aspiration is whether it is *measurable or binary*. Let's test this criterion now: the "no-blame culture" approach fails the binary test as leaders can argue "it wasn't blame; it was accountability."

Zooming back into the case study, how did the Behavioral Standards subgroup avoid this confusion between blame and accountability? Given how often this issue was prioritized, that group created a Behavioral Standard to maximize accountability without driving quality issues underground.

The site's first Behavioral Standard was visually displayed this way:

Behavioral Standards

When things go wrong, we ask:

"What happened?"

"Why did it happen?" and

"How do we prevent it happening again?"

We don't ask:

"Who did it?"

With this Behavioral Standard, feedback can be based on whether the above straightforward sequence happened or not, and therefore meets the binary criterion. Accountability without blame, and no more frustrating Humpty Dumpty debates on the meaning of words!

This issue had been the most frequent behavioral issue I have seen prioritized by employees on Consensus Day. When employees saw it was not only addressed, but was Behavioral Standard Number 1, the message was clear that this was different from their previous experiences.

The power of this Behavioral Standard was demonstrated some months later when a senior corporate quality executive arrived onsite and joined an investigation into a serious quality issue. She knew the site, so she asked, "Whose neck to grab?"

There was a silence in the room as everyone looked to see whether management would defend the local Behavioral Standard when it was being undermined by senior corporate leadership. The operations manager politely explained how RME had changed the way quality issues were investigated. Again, the room fell silent.

The senior quality executive humbly apologized, acknowledged how the site's quality had improved in recent months, and enthusiastically joined in the new approach. The message went out that "management defended our new culture to their big bosses, they are sincere . . . and our big bosses supported us." Culture is created when it is tested in action (see Figure 5.2), and Behavioral Standards set clear and unambiguous expectations for how we respond to those inevitable tests.

Employee Message to RME Visitors: "Cut and Paste Will Disappoint"

Employees on many RME sites proudly conduct visitor tours. Senior visitors often comment that they intend to use these standards when they return to their own organizations. Employee guides explain that "this cannot be rolled out, it has to be created by your employees," but one group felt this was not always understood. Trained in Continuous Improvement, they designed their own polite semi poka-yoke (a method meaning "mistake proofing," ensuring the problem does not reoccur); they attached the following warning on their Behavioral Standards posters and displays: "Warning: attempts to apply these standards without the process that created them will only disappoint!" I recommend this as standards best practice.

Respectful Challenge—
Not Vengeful Denunciation

All RME sets of Behavioral Standards include one standard covering how to prevent the new culture from being undermined. The idea is to respectfully challenge any behavior that undermines the new culture in a spirit of assuming positive intent.

Since I created RME in the 1990s, a worrying societal trend has developed that is the exact opposite of a key component of the Behavioral Standards approach. As if the Enlightenment and the core values of liberal democracies had never happened, and in stark contrast to the charitable and nonjudgmental values inherent in RME, we see highly motivated political activists "call out" others on social media and attempt to damage or end their careers. These activists unilaterally decide if others have infringed newly created ideologies. The spirit is "no mistake must go unpunished, and all intent is negative." It resembles an uncharitable children's movie with the "goodies" doing the denunciation of the rest of us in the role of fallible "baddies."

In contrast, employees designing their own Behavioral Standards often take the hurt and frustrations of being judged and positively redirect that energy into avoiding doing this to others. Given the inevitability of human error, this drives improvement activity rather than recriminations. In achieving the results outlined in these pages, many mistakes were made. Indeed, there is a bias toward trying to do what has never been done before, inevitably generating mistakes along the way. Rational and calculated risk-taking is encouraged; it drives innovation and enhances competitiveness and thus job creation. This approach recognizes that good people make mistakes and takes a charitable and empathetic approach to those mistakes.

Employee facilitators of the Behavioral Standards workshops are supplied with a bespoke facilitator guide to aid consistency and to reduce the burden on the facilitator. A recent guide addressed how to respectfully challenge breaches of the agreed Behavioral Standards:

The spirit of our challenge is that when an individual breaches one of our Behavioral Standards, it is a case of "a good person who made a mistake" and we gently challenge always assuming positive intent. That way we defend our culture, but we do so in a respectful manner consistent with our other Behavioral Standards. Everyone will be given training in how to respectfully challenge to make it easier to have these difficult conversations.

Assuming positive intent also implies trying to engage with the aforementioned activists to explore which approach is more likely to lead to the universally tolerant and respectful society we all aspire to. The majority of activists want to make the world a better place, so the issue is how to get there. Many of the techniques facilitators use for managing conflict work well here. To supplement the work of the external facilitator, and to embed this capacity, internal facilitators are trained in how to use these techniques.

Behavioral Standards Examples

Because ownership creates discretionary effort, each set of Behavioral Standards is codified from the behaviors prioritized by that particular workforce. The examples that follow arise from the unique circumstances and history of the workforces that created them. I am frequently asked, "I know that I shouldn't copy others' Behavioral Standards, but could you give some examples of what other organizations have used?" Here are some examples.

Boston Scientific: "We Won't Do the Wrong Thing to Appear Green"

In a traffic light reporting system, green indicates "on target." Leaders like things to be on target. Making leaders and corporate happy by reporting rose-tinted results ticks the career management box, but it has predictable effects on integrity, innovation, pace of change, and quality of decision-making. To avoid this, Boston Scientific has a Behavioral Standard stating: "We won't do the wrong thing to appear green" (Figure 6.1).

FIGURE 6.1 **Boston Scientific Behavioral Standards (Operations)**

Our Behavioural Standards
OPERATIONS

1. We show respect by taking the time to listen, understand and appreciate each other
2. Assume: positive intent and value in each other
3. We are open to different opinions... and we have the courage to challenge
4. We won't do the wrong thing to appear 'green'
5. Understand, prioritise, commit... and then deliver!
6. See it, Own it, Do it!
7. We have the courage to challenge our own and others':
   - Negative or restrictive assumptions
   - Talking behind anyone's back
   - Deliberate under performance
   - Taking credit for others work
   - Functional and self centred thinking
   - Any breach of Our Standards

Reproduced with kind permission of Boston Scientific.

Stressing his experience of joining Boston Scientific six years after the RME process began, production unit manager Alan Heneghan said:

> In my working experience even in good cultures, when the pressure is on, standards of behavior deteriorate . . . not here. I applied because of what I heard about the culture . . . people referenced "the change" and by God, I could really feel it, instantly. . . . The Behavioral Standards are part of the day-to-day language; in a meeting last week someone said, "let's make sure we don't do the wrong thing to appear green," he didn't look at the wall, it is just part of the culture.

Rolls-Royce and Ballina Beverages (Coca-Cola)

*Remember, in every job that's to be
done there is an element of fun!**
Rolls-Royce

We get work done and still have fun!
Ballina Beverages
Coca-Cola Corp

In 2008, the employees in Experimental Logistics in Rolls-Royce were worried that their Behavioral Standards might be used in a judgmental rather than the kind, developmental way intended. They decided that even difficult conversations are better done with a smile. In March 2020, immediately before the Covid-19 related lockdown, the employees at Ballina Beverages had similar worries about the potential misuse of Behavioral Standards to inhibit the lightheartedness that makes life so much better, so they addressed it in their standards. In both organizations, in different countries 12 years' apart, employees prioritized the desire to derive fun from even the most serious situations.

The OD Perspective: Corporate Values Provide Integration and Behavioral Standards Provide Differentiation

Many corporate leaders worry that Behavioral Standards will undermine their corporate values; this is an understandable concern. An adaptation of the organizational development (OD) concept of integration versus differentiation (Lawrence and Lorsch 1986) is helpful here. Organizational integration is ideal for those aspects of an

---

* Strongly influenced by lyrics of "A Spoonful of Sugar" by Robert B. and Richard M. Sherman, sung by Julie Andrews in *Mary Poppins*.

organization that need to be standardized across different locations; examples include financial reporting standards, capital allocation processes, and corporate values. Key here is "need to be," which is not the same as "would be more convenient to be." Locations differ in culture, history, legal requirements, customer taste, and so on. In contrast, differentiation is required to ensure this local diversity is fully respected in how the organization operates. An example is the diversity in food content in McDonald's restaurants across the world, compared to the service process, which is integrated or standardized.

All organizational structures have advantages and disadvantages; in the absence of awareness of the integration/differentiation distinction, organizations tend to overreact to the inevitable downsides of whatever their current structure is and move too far in the opposite direction. Over-differentiated structures lead to local quality problems or other scandals and/or inappropriate levels of interorganizational competition (to the detriment of shareholder value). Issues with over-integrated structures include the loss of highly innovative and performing leaders. In the latter case, it is crucial to avoid well-intentioned reactions to local scandals causing an overadjustment and a degree of centralization that reduces the solution space of talented executives and incentivizes them to join competitors.

I have seen employee-created visual management processes discarded in a misguided application of standardization. Imagine how proud employees feel when they have created their own visual management design that works well in providing real-time visual data to guide them in their work. Imagine how they feel when someone comes along and discards all their work and imposes a uniform design. Given the technical diversity involved in designing and manufacturing diverse products, these uniform designs are often created in a different technical environment than many employees experience. These "one-size-fits-all" designs thus suboptimize, in that they do not even meet the "technical" aspect of sociotechnical design while blindly undermining ownership and respect. This is a reminder that humility matters, and senior management "thinking they know best" damages engagement.

In summary, establish the optimum balance between integration and differentiation for your organization and avoid lurches between high integration and high differentiation. This is achieved by explicitly and situationally deciding what should be integrated and what needs to be differentiated, thus optimizing both. In the context of RME, Behavioral Standards provide highly sensitive differentiation and supplement, but do not replace, the integration effects of well-designed and communicated corporate values.

How Will My Manager Respond to This New Reality?

Once Behavioral Standards have been created, employees are briefed, by their peers, on the Joint Change Plan to address all the issues they prioritized. At this stage, employees have a set of Behavioral Standards to clarify their new culture. They also know that employee facilitators will be selected in each area and shift and will be trained to run workshops exploring the day-to-day practicalities of the new culture. Their thoughts turn to their managers, and they wonder: "How will my manager react to this new reality?" The next chapter addresses this issue.

Leadership That Moves the Dial

This works far better than any of the many approaches to leadership and engagement I have experienced; it transformed two previously poorly managed sites into best in GB; it just works!

Steve Thorpe
GB operations director, Coca-Cola European Partners

In my corporate career I progressed from a recipient to a purchaser and finally to a designer of leadership development. This was a deeply frustrating journey. Let's explore that frustration and how the outcomes of it will help your organization facilitate and sustain a high-performance culture.

Why Do We Expect So Little from Leadership Development?

As Jim Collins's research demonstrated (Collins 2001), organizations need to decide "first who, then what." How we select and develop leaders matters. A Hult Ashridge Business School survey found that only 7 percent of senior managers believe that their organizations develop leaders effectively (Gitsham 2009). Would you or your organization tolerate such a return on investment for any other expenditure? When I hear comments about a leadership conference or workshop such as "I got one or two ideas" or "it was a good refresher" I despair—what a pathetically low return on the opportunity cost of attending.

Let's aim much higher. Imagine leadership development with systematic follow-up routines and accountability (Collins 2001) delivering comprehensive best practice rather than a few insights. Imagine the aggressive and unsentimental deprioritization, if not systematic elimination, of interventions that absorb the precious time of leaders while adding little practical value. Imagine the impact of implementing 100 percent of a system that had already removed all redundant content and one that focuses on the most effective interventions determined by a strict Pareto analysis statistically calculating the vital few interventions that provide the most impact.* This provides the data to reliably focus on what type of leadership interventions moved the dial the most and, crucially, what interventions can be safely deprioritized. This chapter explains how to achieve that capacity-increasing and time-saving outcome.

In so doing, we minimize what Kahneman and colleagues call "unwanted variation" in leadership outcomes. We do this by systematically countering not just biases but also data quality issues,

---

* Pareto analysis is often simplified as the "80/20" rule; clearly, it is not always 80/20!

diagnostic error, and "noise" or random scatter.* Cumulatively, these are powerful antidotes to groupthink, lack of cognitive diversity, arrogance, and overconfidence.

My focus is the practical needs of busy leaders, and these drive demanding expectations from investment in leadership development. If we do this, we can significantly increase accountability and standards and provide the kind of leadership that a highly engaged and enabled workforce craves and deserves.

Senior leaders who have applied the methodology outlined in this chapter were interviewed about their experiences of the RME approach to leadership. Their feedback provides encouragement that we don't have to accept low expectations. Here are some examples:

- Coca-Cola's Steve Thorpe, GB operations director, Coca-Cola European Partners, said, "This works far better than any of the many approaches to leadership and engagement I have experienced; it transformed two previously poorly managed sites into best in GB; it just works!"
- Looking back at his time as Lake Region Medical's first Continuous Improvement engineer, John O'Dwyer emphasized the leverage effect on improvement efforts, saying, "It provided the DNA of our approach at Lake Region and set the tone for how we facilitated all our lean events. It gave the team leaders the confidence to facilitate our shop floor improvements and to hold senior leaders to account."
- Seagate Technology's Andrew Caldwell, director of product engineering, said, "The best leadership program I've ever experienced. Seriously outstanding and thoroughly enjoyable."
- Paul Whyte, senior manager, operations Continuous Improvement at Stryker, noted: "In both Johnson & Johnson and Boston Scientific we initially didn't understand the

---

* Kahneman, Sibony, and Sunstein 2021 draw an important distinction between bias, which is systematic deviation, and noise, which is random scatter.

variation in effectiveness between the highest and lowest performers in our CI team; we then found a clear correlation between those who used the Cathedral Model (explained later in this chapter) and high performance; this correlation was subsequently repeated more widely among the leadership group."

The leadership system they are describing will be outlined in the second half of this chapter, but first it is useful to diagnose why leadership training has disappointed so many participants and the senior leaders funding it.

Why Do We Tolerate Variation in Leadership Outcomes?

After graduating from the University of Warwick, I joined the highly respected and heavily resourced graduate development programs of first Shell and then Unilever. In both, the model was to find future executives by recruiting the best graduates from elite universities and then giving them intensive development.* Development was via highly comprehensive and structured leadership training with face-to-face exposure to eminent thought leaders. In addition, we were guaranteed rapid, and often cross-functional, changes in job roles to repeatedly accelerate our learning curves and broaden our total business understanding.

I understood the theory but felt uneasy. I knew something was wrong but did not have the experience to anticipate the multiple negative consequences of telling young graduates, already from elite universities, that they were the best of the best before they had achieved anything at work. This entitlement effect was compounded

---

* Completion of Unilever's program gave partial exemption from many prestigious MBA programs.

by giving us superior status and enhanced pay and conditions compared to our nonelite colleagues.

Professional sports has made similar mistakes in creating an entitlement mentality among young players; this is the opposite of what it takes to succeed in elite sports (Syed 2017), or indeed, in any competitive situation. Collaborating intensively with these elite graduates, I worked with some superb people, but also with some of the most narcissistic and entitled individuals I have ever met. I tentatively searched for the root cause of my discomfort with this model. I knew from my experience of competitive sport* that variation is an enemy of consistency. At work, I learned how important minimizing variation was to the quality and productivity of technical equipment. I asked myself two questions:

1. How is it possible to spend so much money on leadership development and yet produce such high levels of unwanted variation in the quality of leadership?
2. Why are we so intolerant of variation in our equipment yet take a laissez-faire attitude to variation in leadership?

The variation in question here is in the quality and quantity of outcomes, unwanted variability in contrast to the natural variation in culture, psychological preference, and individual style, which is healthy. These questions persist to this day. Look around the world and you see superb leadership, but you also see numerous examples of very poor leadership delivered by highly educated and expensively trained leaders. What follows outlines the major findings of that diagnosis; let's start the diagnosis by examining leadership from a customer perspective—how employees experience it.

---

* I currently assess soccer players for the Football Association of Ireland.

How Employees Experience Leadership and Culture

How many times have you heard executives claim that the culture of their organization is one of respect for employees or customer first or innovation and openness to challenge? How can they deliver their avowed culture consistently unless they ensure that every people manager in the organization models the behaviors consistent with that claimed culture?

Given that employees are, in one sense, the customers of leadership, if we tolerate variation in the standards of leadership, how can we prevent the employee experience of the culture being random? If we tolerate and facilitate semi-random inputs, why are we surprised by semi-random outputs?

The combined effect of these semi-random outputs cannot reasonably be called a cohesive culture; it is better described as a nonaligned collection of separate cultural fiefdoms centered on powerful individual departmental or functional heads. Let's diagnose why traditional leadership development has struggled with this issue and has, accidentally, compounded the problem.

Why Does Traditional Leadership Development Suboptimize?

This section outlines some of my key findings when I asked, "Why is leadership development producing such a wide variation in leadership outcomes?" Applying Pareto analysis, the top four causes I found were time interval between usage, unnecessary complexity, overspecialization, and provider capture.

Time Interval Between Usage—the Wayne Rooney Example

In 2009, Wayne Rooney of Manchester United scored an overhead kick in a big soccer game; guess what skill all the UK soccer kids were practicing later that day in the park? How many times in a season will a soccer player use an overhead kick? For people who do not understand soccer, the answer is fewer than 10 times a season. In contrast, a soccer player needs to control the ball, using many parts of the body, many times in every game. Logically, if we want to produce a good soccer team, which of these two skills should we spend more time improving?

When I looked at the content of leadership development programs, I found a disproportionally large coverage of the equivalent of overhead kicks, and far too little time devoted to controlling the ball. We had accidentally neglected the importance of mastering the foundations, those day-to-day conversational skills deployed frequently and well by top leaders.

Unnecessary Complexity

I regularly run workshops where hundreds, sometimes thousands, of employees describe how they see their leaders and their organizations. Employees report that they hear their leaders describe what appear to be the same issues in very different ways. When I investigate, I find that a source of this unwanted variation is the wide range of conceptual models individual leaders use to communicate common themes.

Employees do not report this complexity positively—it is not experienced as welcome cognitive diversity. Rather, I repeatedly hear employees complain of lack of leadership alignment and competence; frequently I hear employees complain that their management "are divided" and "don't know what they are doing."

The RME leadership approach summarized in this chapter addresses this issue head-on by substituting thousands of leadership models with just five models designed to provide a common diagnostic framework and language. One of the five, the Cathedral Higher Purpose Model, will be outlined below.

Overspecialization

To see why overspecialization is a problem, let's compare the contrasting priorities of individuals as they become more senior in academic and organizational careers (Table 7.1).

TABLE 7.1 **Priorities and Sensitivities Necessary for Success: Academic vs. Organizational Executive Careers**

Area	Academic	Executive
Focus	*Deeper and deeper* knowledge of their specialty	*Broader and broader* competencies as responsibility increases over more and more organizational units; legal, political, and cultural systems; and people
Consequence	Advancement of science but decreasing sensitivity to boundary and system issues remote from the deep specialty. This divergence from executive experience is increased as such sensitivity is not necessary for career advancement.	Because systems do not optimize by focus on their parts, executives develop increasing sensitivity to, and skill in, optimizing interrelated systems. This is necessary to achieve organizational success without which career success is unlikely.

Provider Capture

Provider capture is widespread in poorly managed organizations. Examples include IT projects where systems are delivered that are convenient for the provider but infuriating for end users. This is frequently caused by the lack of early end-user engagement in design.* It is present, for example, when public health systems, which require a 24-7 service, contract doctors and other specialists on a Monday-through-Friday basis, covering weekends with voluntary overtime. This failure to ensure *the right numbers of the right specialists at the right time* in hospitals means that patients die unnecessarily.†

---

* The introduction of a highly visible end-user engagement process was an important outcome from one of the Rolls-Royce RMEs.

† On a sad personal note, my own mother died during a holiday weekend in a small hospital where every doctor declined to work overtime that weekend.

Provider capture partially explains why some health system managers allow doctors to book skiing holidays in winter and then complain to the media about a "winter crisis." Winter is predictable, and the fact that it happens does not lead to crisis in well-run health systems.

The same phenomenon happens in leadership development when what the market offers organizations is convenient and revenue-enhancing for the provider but suboptimizes the value added for the user. As an example, let's examine a case study in producer capture.

Case Study in Provider Capture: The Coaching Market

You read earlier that I assess interventions on how effective they are. If they don't add enough competitive advantage, they are either halted, reduced in priority, or alternative approaches are tried and tested until the dial moves. Coaching fell into that third category as it delivered some results in some circumstances, but the gap with its potential impact was large.

What causes this gap between coaching's potential and its actual organizational impact? Many professional coaches sell their services in hourly or daily segments. They tend to coach one-on-one with executives. The coaching interventions are not usually integrated into a wider leadership system, nor are they designed to systematically leverage Continuous Improvement learning and techniques.

This "set piece" coaching approach is organized in advance, limited in duration, and focuses on a small proportion of leaders. When done well, it is value-adding, especially for executives. This minority model of coaching is core to the multiplying professional qualifications regarded as prerequisites within the coaching profession. A major downside is that scaling this model to all leaders is unaffordable for most organizations. Coaching becomes an elite, minority activity with corresponding diminution of its organizational impact. Coaching is *rationed by cost*.

There is an alternative: if you reframe coaching from a minority and set piece activity to an across-the-organization activity embedded in the daily repetitive systems and routines that drive improvement, it will leverage those systems and routines. If coaching is seen as part of an integrated system of leadership, this further increases the multiplier effects. Crucially, increasing the capability of all leaders and all employees, not just a minority of senior leaders, is affordable for even the smallest organizations.

This alternative, mass approach to coaching is much less lucrative for providers, as once all managers, and sometimes all employees, learn to coach and how to continuously improve their practice, there is a limited future income stream for the provider. The commercial interests of the provider conflict with the best interests of the customer, but customers are not aware of what is possible, so they accept the market status quo. This case study aims to destabilize that comfort with the status quo. A more detailed exploration of these different approaches follows in the coaching section.

Setting Higher Expectations for Leaders

Having outlined why conventional leadership development has suboptimized, let's examine opportunities to set our leadership expectations higher, to demonstrate what is possible in how we develop our leaders.

The Vision

In setting expectations, "100 percent implementation" and "systematic" are key concepts; we are not playing at leadership; our employees deserve demanding standards for the leaders who so centrally impact their lives and careers. At the organizational level, we must create a culture where no employee hesitates to apply for a job because of worries about the behavior or capability of their prospective manager. We need to have the evidence-based trust in our leadership systems to confidently set expectations for that employee about all leaders in our organization; we need to be able to say:

Never worry about who the boss is when you apply for a job here; all our leaders will develop you to the best of your abilities, none will take you for granted and all will challenge and stretch you while actively managing overcommitment; all will be there for you, just like your current boss is. Leaders who don't meet this standard consistently don't remain long as leaders here.

The meticulous, detailed, unsexy, daily routines necessary to have that evidence-based confidence are outlined in the following section.

Words Frame Expectations

Terminology matters because it frames expectations. Replacing the term "training" with "preparation for action" signals that quick application and improvements are expected. Another change is to reduce isolated development of individual leaders who have little chance to make improvements, and instead implement systematic, collective improvement in outputs. This is less commercially valuable for suppliers but results in much more return on investment for the customer. We should not accept "I gained a few insights" as an output from a learning event. We need to implement 100 percent of the system and skills selected to move the dial. In this alternative approach, the clear expectation is that you will be held accountable multidirectionally, by your own team, your peers, and your boss; to apply what you have learned systematically using the disciplines and methodologies provided. The accountability will be skilled and gentle at first but also includes the tools to quickly accelerate the learning of slow learners where necessary.

The multiple and multidirectional accountability mechanisms are key differentiators for the Cathedral Higher Purpose Model (CHPM). Meggitt's Danielle White, director of process excellence, stressed this point when she said, "I have attended many leadership programs in different organizations; they all scratch the surface compared to the Cathedral Model."

A New Standard: "Model and Reference"

As RME is implemented it is crucial that leaders at all levels systematically "model and reference" the new culture and leadership approach. "Model" simply means leading by personal example. "Reference" is more complex. If we lead by example but don't join the dots, individuals soon take the new culture for granted, demonstrating the old proverb that "eaten bread is soon forgotten." To avoid this, leaders must regularly provide historical context. This refreshes people's memory of the significant changes made by RME, its bottom-up nature, and how the Behavioral Standards and changes in policies and procedures were achieved. The linkages to employees' own RME decisions are crucial here, and they become more so as the success in creation of new jobs dilutes the percentage of leaders and employees who participated in the original RME process.

Donald Duck and Personal Variation

I am often challenged by leaders who make the reasonable point that we are not the same every day or every part of every day. This is true but not a reason for dropping our standards.

As leaders we cast a leader's shadow; everything we do and don't do, everything we say and don't say is watched and interpreted by employees. If you are a leader and you walk past an employee in a corridor without acknowledging the employee's existence as a human being, what shadow do you think you have created? A realistic personal standard is to say to yourself each day: "Yes, sometimes we all feel less than 100 percent, but what our employees experience must be highly consistent; I never want someone to approach my PA or colleagues and ask: 'What kind of mood is he or she in?'"

When we take our kids to Disney World, we don't expect to go around a corner and find Donald Duck with his head under his arm having a cigarette! The mindset is: "Just like Donald Duck in Disney World, I will not disappoint the expectations people have of me. I will stay in character, the character we expect of our leaders." Now that we have set high expectations, we also need to determine what specific leadership interventions, in which specific combinations and sequences, are most likely to work in practice.

Pareto Analysis on Improving Performance

From my background in soccer, I knew that certain attributes made players statistically more likely to succeed. I then discovered that the Venn diagrams for elite sports and organizational performance overlap but do not coincide.* I wondered if there are some generic leadership skills that improve performance of individuals, teams, and organizations, and if so, how do we discover what they are? Thus began a 40-year and counting search for what works. What follows details the emergent outcome of a very large Pareto analysis that continues to this day.

This Pareto ranked interventions according to the extent they "moved the dial" by making tangible positive differences in productivity, quality, engagement, enablement, and so on. I then looked for a natural Pareto breakpoint where the *absolute* difference in effectiveness justified separating what was included from what was deprioritized. I sought the cutoff point beyond which the opportunity cost of inclusion was greater than the value of the intervention. Leaders are the end users here, and their feedback on what is working is crucial but has often not been heard well by the designers of leadership training. Compounding this problem, many individual leaders, protective of their careers and keen to manage upward, often judge that this is not a hill to die on. The outcome is often resigned compliance or passionate lip service rather than the 100 percent openness and commitment needed for success in any learning environment.

---

* I later discovered that neither fully coincides with success in the miliary despite crucial and applicable learning from that inspirational source.

FIGURE 7.1 **The Cathedral Higher Purpose Model**

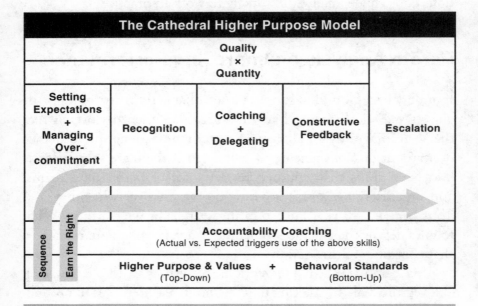

When leaders see the Cathedral Higher Purpose Model illustrated in Figure 7.1, I am often asked, "Why does your Cathedral Model cover the significance of recognition but specifically exclude reward? Why is appraisal excluded?" Reward and appraisal feature prominently in conventional leadership development programs; they matter and must be managed, but I could not find enough return on investment to justify focus on them at the expense of higher-impact interventions. The phrase "Reward and Recognition" is unhelpful here as it combines high-impact and low-impact interventions into a conceptually meaningless average. A key deliverable is to create leadership capacity or time to focus on those key interventions diagnosed by strict prioritization; this is diluted if low-impact interventions such as reward are not actively deprioritized.

Let's look at appraisal as an example of what has been deprioritized. A few years ago, I looked at the total expenditure in the UK training market on appraisal compared to the spending on three key day-to-day leadership skills, namely recognition, coaching, and constructive feedback. In that year, the United Kingdom spent more on appraisal training than on all three day-to-day leadership skills combined. Why is that finding significant?

In an average year, how many times does a good leader move the dial with appraisal? In the same year, how many times does a good leader move the dial with recognition, coaching, and constructive feedback? So why spend more on appraisal?

If we systematically ensure that no employee is taken for granted, that the quality of recognition is high, that coaching is a cultural norm with spontaneous unplanned coaching maximizing development and ownership of ideas, and that if something goes off track it is immediately but skillfully addressed through constructive feedback, how easy will the appraisal conversations be? That is why appraisal did not make the Pareto cutoff point for inclusion. The nature of Pareto is that some interventions will move the dial more reliably, more powerfully, and more often than others. Recognition made the cutoff point—reward and appraisal did not. In summary, the practical lesson for leaders is that if you try to prioritize everything, nothing will be done well enough to give you a competitive advantage. Instead, *systematically prioritize* above the Pareto breakpoint and, *at most*, simply manage interventions below that point.*

The key to doing this well is changing the way we frame leadership. The transformation is from seeing leadership as a collection of unrelated specialties to seeing leadership as a system.

Leadership as a System

Martin Lunn, Aptiv's global OPEX director, stressed the criticality of framing leadership as a system when he said:

---

* My Pareto may change over time; I also welcome data from other researchers to increase my accumulated sample size to test ongoing validity and to make further improvements.

Other leadership approaches provide separate jigsaw pieces which tend to fall apart due to the lack of the integrated system, designed easy-to-remember simplicity, daily routines, and values foundation which make the Cathedral Model core skills approach so effective. In a world of knowledge and concept overload, this provides a concise and clear answer to the question of "what" leaders should focus on.

When I experimented, I found that systems effects mattered. Key examples were that, as in medicine and other fields, the same interventions done in different sequences produced different outcomes and that some interventions are counterproductive if applied in the absence of others, but effective in combination.* We will examine some examples as we explore the model in detail.

The Cathedral Higher Purpose Model

Why did I initially call this system of leadership the Cathedral Model? The first reason was that in the 1990s, leaders in the diagnostic and problem-solving/data-literate intellectual stream were familiar with the visualization of key operational and quality concepts as buildings with columns (see Hauser and Clausing 1988; this was also how the Toyota Production System, and many derivatives of it, were illustrated). I wanted to reduce barriers by talking in the language and the images of my key stakeholders, most of whom inhabited the diagnostic and problem-solving intellectual stream.†

The second reason is because of a story. The story goes that a visitor to a building site looked down into an excavation and asked one

---

* An example is constructive feedback in the absence of prior investment in recognition, coaching, and managing overcommitment. See the "earning the right" arrow in the CHPM.
† Similarly, it is important to talk in the language of, and understand the history of, trade unions when communicating employee engagement concepts to understandably skeptical union representatives.

bricklayer what he was doing. The bricklayer replied, "I'm laying bricks, what do you think I'm doing?"

The visitor then asked the same question of a second bricklayer. This time, the response was "I am building a cathedral."

Many leaders see the logical significance of the second bricklayer's response, namely that he sees the big picture and where his work fits within it. Many leaders miss the emotional aspect of his response, his pride in his work. When Matt Reddick left Amazon in 2022, his colleagues showed they understood and appreciated his commitment to the cathedral story with the farewell gift shown in Figure 7.2.

FIGURE 7.2 "HERE'S TO THE FUTURE OF BUILDING CATHEDRALS"

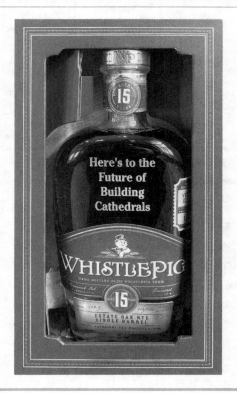

Reproduced with kind permission of Matt Reddick.

That pride and ownership shown by Matt's team is key to employee engagement and to understanding leadership as a system, not merely a collection of separate skills and interventions. Let's build the model, section by section, starting with its foundation and then working left to right as illustrated in Figure 7.3.

FIGURE 7.3 **The Cathedral Model Foundation Level**

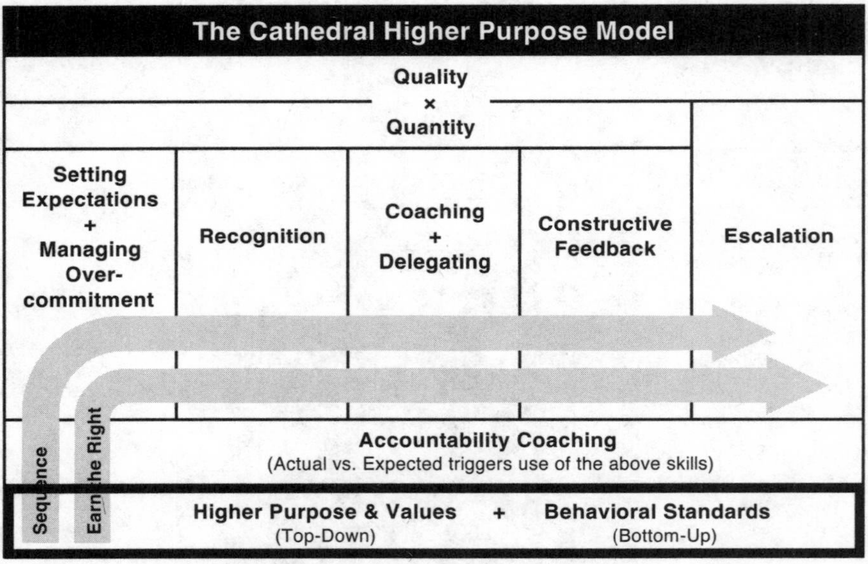

The Cathedral Higher Purpose Model

		Quality × Quantity		
Setting Expectations + Managing Over-commitment	Recognition	Coaching + Delegating	Constructive Feedback	Escalation

Accountability Coaching
(Actual vs. Expected triggers use of the above skills)

Higher Purpose & Values + **Behavioral Standards**
(Top-Down)   (Bottom-Up)

Sequence   *Earn the Right*

The Foundation Level

In the Foundation Level, the "Higher Purpose" reference reminds leaders to connect to employees via a meaningful Higher Purpose. It reminds leaders that work is more than just earning a living, that work also creates jobs and prevents forced emigration from those communities historically blighted by it. It visually signals that leaders are custodians who seek to pass on better jobs and more prosperity to future generations in the same way that parents seek a better life for their children. It elevates the ambition for leaders from caretakers to those who improve what they inherit.

The "Values" reference links to the organization's own values and can be mapped against those values to deliver organization integration as well as local differentiation (Lawrence and Lorsch 1986). It also signals the implicit values inherent in a philosophy that looks for and finds the good in people and seeks to remove artificial but common restrictions on employees' growth and development. These values impact how the skills above them in the model are applied.

The phrase "Behavioral Standards" reminds all leaders that the leadership skills depicted above the Foundation Level are implemented in such a way that they align with RME's employee-created culture. This is a visual signal that the individual leadership skills do not flourish in isolation in their inward-looking silos but are part of a systems sequence; they are not a random collection of separate specialties.

The parenthetical "bottom-up" explains how the high-performance culture was agreed and codified by the workforce itself. This reminds leaders of the extent of solution space inherent in the RME culture. Let's now start the model's left-to-right sequence of leadership skills by ensuring everyone knows exactly what is expected of them without being exploited.

Setting Expectations and Managing Overcommitment

The first leadership pillar addresses Setting Expectations and Managing Overcommitment (Figure 7.4).

Setting Expectations

Gallup's Q12 Employee Engagement Survey starts by checking to what extent employees agree with "I know what is expected of me at work." I am frequently surprised by how many employees' motivation, focus, and efficiency are negatively impacted by lack of clarity in this respect.

In the model, senior leaders align horizontally by mutually agreeing what they expect from each other. Then this alignment

FIGURE 7.4 **Setting Expectations and Managing Overcommitment**

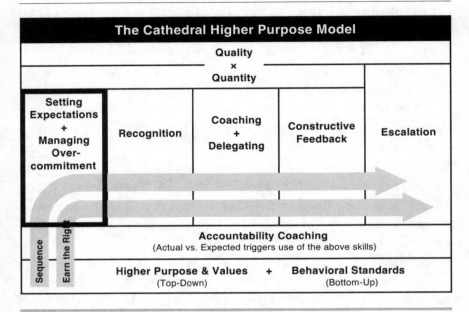

is cascaded down and across the organization in a bespoke manner designed to leverage the results of Policy Deployment. Despite the cascade, hierarchy is minimized, which powerfully reinforces respect, teamwork, and mutuality. Such mutuality sets the scene for the joint evaluation of workload in the second part of this pillar, "Managing Overcommitment."

Managing Overcommitment

How do we treat employees who habitually offer extensive discretionary effort? These employees often are reluctant to say no, or to disappoint anyone asking them to do work; they tend commit to do the work and only afterward assess the amount of work required to deliver the commitment.

Lazy managers will often just accept the commitment from the employee and assume that as that employee has always delivered in the past, he or she will deliver on this new commitment. The employee concerned tends to simply increase her or his workload, often by first increasing the lengths of days, then gradually eroding weekends.

Imagine this scenario: An overcommitted employee does not arrive one morning for a meeting. Everyone is surprised as it is out of character, but everyone is relieved when she arrives 45 minutes later embarrassed for sleeping through her alarm.

A few weeks later, she again sleeps when she should be awake, but this time, she is driving home one night after a very long week and falls asleep at the wheel, killing herself and a family coming in the opposite direction.

In both cases the organization's toleration of the employee's overcommitment led to oversleeping; in the first case she slept in the safety of her bed and did not hear her alarm; in the second case she fell asleep while driving her car. The only difference in the outcome was luck. No lessons were learned after the first incident, and the luck ran out for that employee and that family on that road that night.

No organization that aims to operate based on values can tolerate such random outcomes. The example above could have been avoided. Why did the employee's boss and others not see her uncharacteristic lateness as a warning? Why did they see it only in retrospect? What happens to the moral basis of the implicit contract between the organization and the employee if employees voluntarily giving more and more discretionary effort are simply taken for granted and overworked?

To avoid acting contrary to our claimed values, we must actively manage overcommitment; it is not enough to provide resilience training or other symptom treatment interventions, we must "predict and prevent" (see Figure I.2) and stop the overcommitment at the source. We do this by establishing mutual expectations between the commitment-seeker and the commitment-giver so that the cumulative impact of employees' workload is calculated and adjusted. Often this involves the systematic challenging of wasteful, gold-plated specifications.* Frequently these conversations produce significant work allocation changes within teams. In this way, managing overcommitment, counterintuitively for some leaders, increases—not reduces—the performance of both individuals and teams. By so doing we not only prevent random (and therefore, potentially catastrophic) failure, but protect the moral basis on which the new culture sits, a key aspect of a sustained high-performance culture.

When we apply the strict Pareto that created the CHPM we focus on a small number of key interventions and actively stop or de-emphasize others. In that way the *fundamental design of the model* also reduces overcommitment. The principle is:

> Discover, using data, what moves the dial and then deliver a small number of key things at high quality and quantity while aggressively challenging non-core activities.

Recognition

Having set clear and mutual expectations and protected against overcommitment, we now need to ensure that no employee is taken for granted, the Recognition pillar in the model (Figure 7.5). All the skills pillars in the model rest on a values foundation, and for Recognition, this differentiates the approach from much conventional recognition training.

For years leaders have been told that the purpose of giving recognition is to encourage the repetition of already positive behaviors. This is why recognition or appreciation are sometimes referred to as "reinforcement feedback." This as a conceptual confusion between one of many positive consequences of recognition, namely reinforcement, and its purpose.

Why do you rush to the aid of an old lady who falls in the street? Not because you want to be included in her will, but because it is

---

* For example, in one case I asked, "As the passengers will be going past these tunnel walls at speed in the dark, why do we need such aesthetically beautiful but expensive and difficult-to-maintain paint?"

FIGURE 7.5 **Recognition**

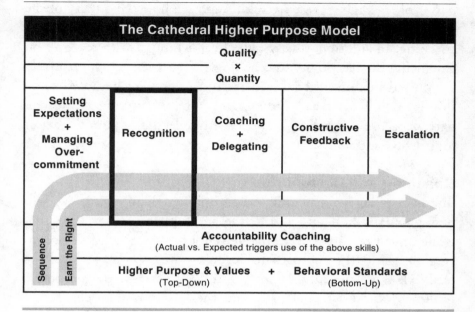

the right thing to do. It is unconditional; we do not do it to get anything back.

Similarly, in the CHPM we give recognition because it is the right thing to do; it is unconditional. This is an example of how the values in the foundation govern the way the leadership skill is deployed. The values determine the approach. When I follow up on the deployment of recognition, employees tell me they notice; they say they feel the difference when someone recognizes them unconditionally compared to their experience when managers wanted something in return. When managers use the Accountability Coaching skill (covered later in this chapter), they report similar responses.

Many leaders experience disappointment when their recognition programs fail to meet expectations; in isolation these programs tend to suboptimize (see below), but as part of a system, recognition leverages and helps earn the right to deploy the other skills in the model. In the coaching section that follows you will discover the power of leveraging these two skills and see how the quality of the recognition itself is enhanced and kept fresh via the stretch effect of coaching. In addition, this system effect is mutual with recognition enhancing the receptivity to coaching. These leverage opportunities are missed in conventional leadership development because leadership is rarely framed as a system, and systems thinking is unusual, partly because it inhabits the opposite intellectual stream to that of most L&D specialists.

Coaching and Delegating

The next pillar is Coaching and Delegating (Figure 7.6). We will now gradually build up and define an approach to coaching that is significantly different from conventional approaches. Prior to creating the RME approach to coaching, in response to local site feedback that "coaching is not working," I asked managers across multiple locations to tell me about the last time they coached. I noticed a strange phenomenon: the majority were using the word "coaching" in a highly unscientific manner, confusing it with training, instructing, and other related concepts where the manager was predominantly in "tell" rather than "ask" mode. This conceptual confusion meant that rather than coaching "not working" as had been reported, in practice it had not been seriously attempted; it lacked a scientific definition of terms.

What types of practical takeaways did practitioners of this coaching approach stress in their interviews? For Suntory's European sustainability director, Keith Allen, it was the practical impact, how tangible it was; for Richard Kallee, Sinter Group's COO, it was the "combination of the scientific method and emotional intelligence." In some RME implementations (including Bacardi, ICBF, and Promed), all employees, not only managers, are trained in coaching and the other CHPM skills. There are multiple competitive advantages when employees as well as managers exploit the many coaching opportunities that arise daily in any workplace. When everyone learns to coach, employees welcome being coached as it

FIGURE 7.6 **Coaching and Delegating**

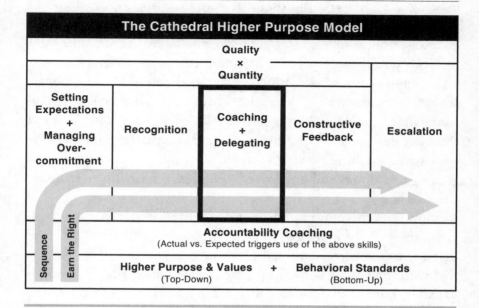

becomes "part of the way we do things around here"; in turn this makes coaching conversations more productive, less hierarchical, and more skilled as the nominal coach is in a conversation with others who understand the process.

Framing coaching as a universal development process rather than a remedial process produces a disproportionately large impact on an often-neglected group—high performers. This group is often assumed "not to need coaching," a bizarre logic for such a powerful developmental skill. Coaching high performers delivers a disproportionately high return on the finite investment of busy managers' time; in contrast, when coaching is seen as remedial (even appearing in disciplinary procedures), employees feel that coaching implies they are not performing—and this reduces their receptivity to being coached.*

---

* Check your organization's disciplinary procedure or equivalent for this confused framing of coaching.

Widespread and systematic coaching also powerfully leverages existing Continuous Improvement activities (see Figure I.2).* In addition, coaching skills enhance multiple organizational events at all levels, from simple conversations to enhancing the scientific rigor of diagnosis. This creates wide and deep competitive advantage.

Delegating is located with coaching in the model. The rationale is that, when done well, delegation creates developmental opportunities that flow down the organization. These opportunities meet the increased capability and confidence of employees unleashed by systematic coaching flowing up the organization: meaningful work is delegated down and employees' confidence flows up to embrace these opportunities.

How does this approach differ from conventional coaching models? Table 7.2 summarizes the deliberate conceptual and practical break with many conventional coaching practices.

In summary, the conventional set piece one-on-one coaching is valuable, but the dial moves much more quickly when every leader is trained in the RME form of coaching outlined in Table 7.2. Key is incorporating systematic data literacy and statistically rigorous problem-identification and problem-solving techniques. By doing this we systematically ensure diagnostic rigor and learn from the known most common errors we all make.

Deep understanding of the Double Diamond model is a key outcome of Phase 2 of the leadership program used in most RME implementations. Double-Diamond coaching is illustrated in Figure 7.7.

When examining the effectiveness of conventional coaching models, I found significant variability in outcomes. In contrast, the Double Diamond approach improved diagnostic quality by systematically removing the main sources of error identified in the original Pareto and subsequently extended by Kahneman's work. Doing this improved the effectiveness, and thus the credibility, of coaching in

---

* As an example, imagine the multiplier effect of a workforce universally skilled in coaching applying Rother's Kata approach. See Rother 2010.

TABLE 7.2 **How Double Diamond Coaching Differs from Conventional Coaching**

Issue	From	To
When/position	Sit-down meeting	Often standing
Status	Often formal	Overwhelmingly informal
Setting	Often a meeting scheduled on calendar	Overwhelmingly opportunistic in the place of work during "normal" events
Continuity	Continuous: driven by the need to adhere to scheduled calendar events; continues to problem-solving even when adequate diagnosis is impossible	Discontinuous: breaking off to "go see"/measure/verify as appropriate; diagnosis first, only then problem-solving
Time elapsed	Often expands to meet time available in calendar!	Often quick, sometimes only one or two diagnostic questions are enough before more data is gathered
Participants	Usually one-on-one	Often one to many, whoever is present
Relationship to problem-solving	None. In practice, unstructured and unscientific problem-solving is often attempted even when adequate diagnosis is impossible	Systematically integrated with structured problem-solving approaches; diagnosis first, only then problem-solving

the eyes of those leaders whose hard science background caused understandable doubt about the effectiveness of coaching.

End-user credibility is also enhanced by applying proven improvement techniques such as visual management: you may have noticed that the top diamond is drawn bigger than the bottom one; this visually reminds users that the top diamond is a danger zone, where more known and predictable errors occur. This acts as an antidote to rushing to solution mode before accurate diagnosis. The latter is itself a common error linked to Kahneman's "thinking fast" concept.

The model also widens the appreciation of the limits of analysis and the value of experimentation. When applied to complex situations, the Double Diamond approach often involves the use of multiple inexpensive experiments rather than being content to

FIGURE 7.7 **The Double Diamond Model**

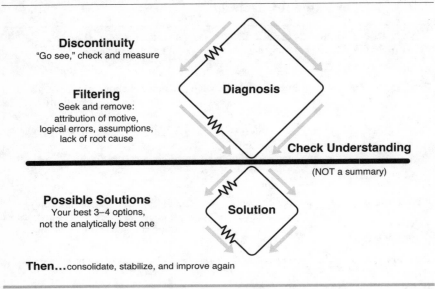

implement the analytically "best" solution, which is sometimes not the best when applied in practice. This adds credibility in the eyes of scientists, engineers, doctors, and others whose work is tested every day by reality, in battle, in our skies, and in our hospitals.

Changing the Coaching Paradigm

When coaching is seen as a key skill for all leaders, it becomes end user focused and is part of everyday organizational life; this overcomes the inevitable limitations of relying on a tiny minority of expensively trained coaches whose numerical insignificance renders them incapable of moving the dial. The vision is for your organization to operate a practical, inexpensive, widely available, ideally universal, and explicitly nonhierarchical coaching approach. This both facilitates and drives Continuous Improvement, high standards, and competitive advantage. Let's examine an example of how coaching and recognition mutually enhance each other.

Systems Leverage Example: Coaching × Recognition

Earlier we explored the CHPM as a dynamic system. The recognition-coaching dynamic is an example of this. Many leaders have approached me to talk through a frustration they have with recognition, saying something like:

> I understand the quality aspect of recognition and that is working well. But the quantity aspect? You have explained "if it is not sincere don't do it," but I struggle to find enough genuine opportunities to give recognition compared to how often I see you do it.

Looking at the CHPM, these leaders see their frustration as a quantity of recognition issue. When I am asked this, I ask leaders the following series of questions:

- If you give team members or colleagues genuine sincere recognition, what happens to their self-esteem?
- As their self-esteem increases, what happens to their confidence?
- As they become more confident, what happens to their receptivity to inputs such as coaching?
- As they become more and more receptive, for any given input, what happens to how much they learn?
- If you see them applying what they have learned, either by doing something they were already doing better, or by doing something well that they hadn't done before, what happens to your natural and spontaneous opportunity to give them recognition?

Leaders quickly conclude that the quantity of genuine sincere recognition is driven up by increasing the quality and quantity of coaching, which is one of the reasons why so many purely recognition schemes suboptimize. Similarly, confident people will be more receptive to coaching, so a dynamic virtuous cycle can be created by the interplay of the two skills delivered in tandem. Finally, integrating recognition and coaching into the daily standard work of leaders will increase both the quantity—because the number of opportunities is so great—and quality of both recognition and coaching.

Constructive Feedback

Moving rightward in the model away from the powerful combination of recognition and coaching, we come to the Constructive Feedback pillar (Figure 7.8). Let's start with some conceptual clarity: coaching and constructive feedback are often applied as if they were the same—they are not; each skill was developed for a particular range of situations and correspondingly will suboptimize if applied inappropriately. A simplified guide is that coaching optimizes when the goal is to further improve already high performance, but sometimes the urgency and/or seriousness of the situation requires a more assertive and quicker intervention. For the latter, constructive feedback may be appropriate. There are subtleties and exceptions, but they are beyond the scope of this book.

Discussing constructive feedback, Boston Scientific's Enda Colleran, director, project management office (APAC region), remembered the transition from previous practice as "we moved from comfortable lies to (initially) unpleasant truths." In the training, the idea that constructive feedback is negative is quickly debunked. This encourages quick, nonjudgmental conversations to "nip any issues in the bud." Constructive feedback may not always be sufficient, or it may be inappropriate due to the severity of the situation. In such situations, a more robust response is required. That is why the fifth pillar is Escalation.

Escalation

The next pillar includes both informal and formal escalation (Figure 7.9). Catastrophizing of legal and reputational risks is prevented, which increases managers' confidence to escalate formally when appropriate. Systems improvements include shortening and simplifying existing HR policies and procedures in this area. This

FIGURE 7.8 Constructive Feedback

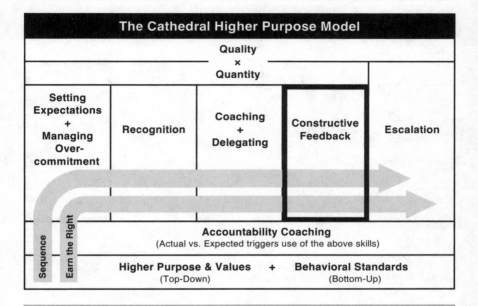

makes the latter more end user friendly, and increases the mutual understanding and empathy between HR and line managers.

Quality × Quantity

Imagine every leader had superb skill levels in all the key skills. What difference would they make if they very rarely used these skills in conversations with employees? If you ring your elderly mother once a week and have a lovely conversation, but that is the only call she gets each week, she is still lonely. Quantity matters.

The literature tends to focus on skill quality, but the unsexy, repetitive, muscle memory disciplines are crucial to improving standards. As an example, it does not matter if a professional tennis player has a world-beating forehand if he cannot move quickly enough into a position where it can be used often enough to win games; it is the tiny daily increases in speed off the mark and stamina that will get the player into those positions often enough to use his forehand. This

FIGURE 7.9 **Escalation**

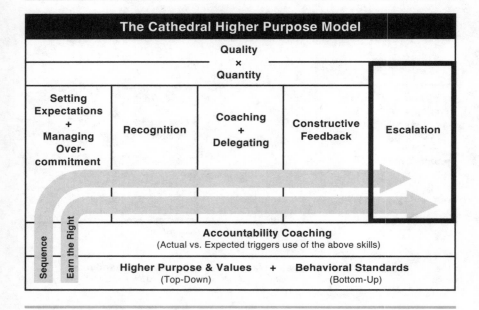

unsexy aspect of excellence bores many external leadership trainers who prefer the exciting material that participants also prefer. These trainers often avoid making their customers uncomfortable by not insisting on accountability, necessary repetition, focus, and daily improvements.

The Quality × Quantity section (Figure 7.10) emphasizes daily relentless passion for improvement; it reminds us that while the quality of the conversation matters, so does the number of conversations. It thus reinforces Continuous Improvement methods such as leader standard work (LSW) that, among other things, ensure enough time is allocated to the important longer-term activity rather than reactively firefighting.*

---

* For those interested in learning more about LSW, the Lean Enterprise Academy, AllAboutLean, and the Lean Enterprise Institute all provide easily accessible outlines.

FIGURE 7.10 **Quality × Quantity**

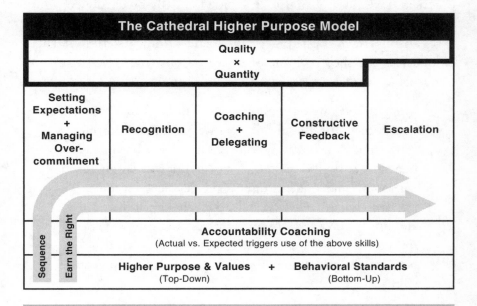

Many trends in business, from increasing spans of control to giving frontline leaders administrative work previously done by administrative staff, have reduced the average number of conversations managers have with individual team members. Imagine if we took the same attitude to sports teams? Imagine if we said to a team sports star, "Hey, while you are making those runs in the game, could you cut the grass and paint the lines!"

The key is to focus on improving both the quality and the quantity of those conversations and resisting trends in the opposite direction. These trends tend to originate when decision-making is based on what can be measured easily such as number of managers, rather than less easy to measure competitive drivers such as the number and quality of conversations with each employee. A similar mistake may be happening post Covid-19, as the tangible costs of property and travel trump the intangible benefits of employees being physically present to create teamwork, social capital, learning, and innovation. The downsides of alienating employees via lack of practical flexibility must also be avoided, ideally by deeply engaging employees on these issues.

Learning from best practice in education, Jozef Butterfield emphasizes the sheer volume of conversations that have driven the remarkable results in his school:

> More unusual are our multiple duties throughout the week; we optimize the amount of time we are around our pupils conversing with them every lunchtime, every break and on frequent stairwell duties. This is in addition to family lunch where staff and students discuss the day's chosen topic. We ask them about their weekends, their thoughts, their hopes, and dreams. We show genuine interest and care which they reciprocate in the classroom. This is central to creating the buy-in from pupils they need to fully reach their potential. (Birbalsingh 2020)

In summary, leadership is a contact sport, and the amount of contact matters.

Let's see how to sustain and grow the skills in the model.

Accountability Coaching

It is often said that "practice makes perfect," but if you practice poor quality, you get well-practiced poor quality. It is perfect practice that makes perfect, and Accountability Coaching (Figure 7.11) is both a process and a skill designed to make systematic and successive approximations toward that goal.

Accountability Coaching is not the same as coaching; it is designed to sustain the gains made by the initial mass engagement, the investment in leadership development, and the application of a Continuous Improvement system. It is also designed to continuously improve the application of leadership skills and adherence to any other standard such as quality or financial standards.

The Accountability Coaching process does this through the leader verifying process, that is, systematically following up on

FIGURE 7.11 Accountability Coaching

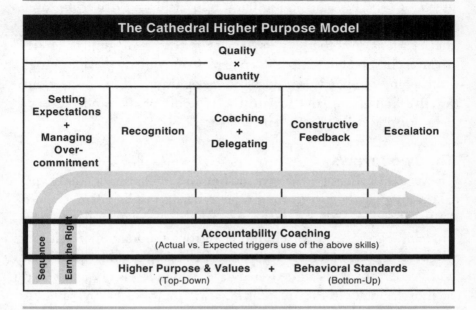

previously established expectations by comparing what was expected to happen with what actually happened. These conversations, gently (at first) nudge toward meeting those standards. This is done while ensuring that leaders are "managing on green," that is, ensuring that the positive aspects of performance are recognized as well as moving forward on any underperformance. The goal is to create an environment where employees know that any conversation with their managers will be a rounded discussion on progress that shows appreciation and empathy for any difficulties in the situation.

Managing on Green

As a corporate leader I found that the "managing on green" aspect of Accountability Coaching was a rich source of information on how corporate initiatives are working when they encounter the reality of the routine work of employees. It also enhanced humility as my idealized optimism about the quality of my corporate initiatives clashed with the realities of frontline challenges. If we "manage on green," that clash can be mutually respectful and drive improvements in both directions while narrowing the gap between HQ and the locations. Another system benefit is that managing on green uncovers best practice and hidden heroes who quietly prevent things from going wrong; this guides our recognition efforts away from reactive firefighting and toward the type of "predict and prevent" behavior that drives improvement.

The Two Arrows

The model includes two arrows starting in the Foundation level and continuing left to right through the leadership skills pillars (Figure 7.12). The first arrow demonstrates the *sequential* nature of the model. Progress starts with building a strong foundation of a shared Higher Purpose, based on Values and Behavioral Standards. It then adds leadership skills all delivered at very high levels of quality and quantity. Finally, these are continuously improved by the application of Accountability Coaching.

The second arrow indicates the need to "earn the right." It is not enough to deliver individual skills *in isolation*; the model is a system, and by working on the Foundation Level and on the left side of it, leaders "earn the right" to move rightward in the model and become more assertive and directional where appropriate. This explains why the same skill delivered to exactly the same standard will "land" differently depending upon prior conversations.

The principle can be summarized as "Don't go near Escalation unless you have earned the right by modeling Behavioral Standards, setting clear and achievable expectations, showing appreciation for the good work being done, coaching your team to maximize potential, and trying to nip any problem in the bud with constructive feedback."

FIGURE 7.12 The Two Arrows

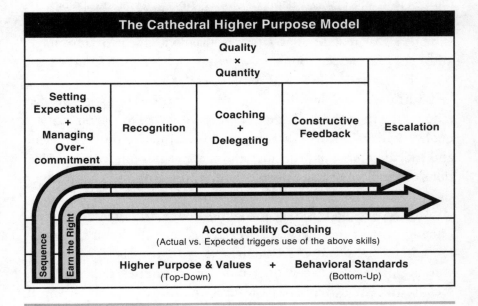

Let Your Leaders Lead

Over many years organizations have sought to cut costs by removing administrative roles and absorbing this work into the frontline leader role. If we burden the people who most directly impact the experience, development, and engagement of our employees, what do we expect to happen to employee engagement? As we saw above, we don't expect our sports stars to cut the grass while playing!

The unintended consequences of loading frontline leaders with administrative tasks include the loss of starter jobs that had historically given those who are practically minded opportunities to prove what they can do. In addition, both cognitive and social diversity have been reduced as avenues to social mobility are accidentally cut off in the name of cost cutting.* Lack of social mobility itself is a danger to the social cohesion on which liberal democratic societies depend; if individuals see themselves as victims, as hopelessly disadvantaged, this reduces motivation to overcome those disadvantages and generates susceptibility to extreme political movements from both the left and right.

Earlier we saw how loading administrative tasks on leaders reduces the time the individual leader can devote to the quantity of quality conversations. Perhaps we could rethink this multiyear trend and provide more opportunities and more routes into our organizations by employing more people in administrative roles from which they can progress.

Why repeat the mistakes made in some police forces and in the nursing profession where unnecessary academic barriers to entry prevent talented and practical people with the right traits from entering professions? Providing more opportunities creates a more socially and cognitively diverse leadership cadre and bench strength, and it prevents scope creep and the consequent dilution of key deliverables. It provides a powerful focus on what "moves the dial" rather than on what is currently politically fashionable.

In summary, creating an employee-owned Continuous Improvement culture changes the role of leadership. Senior leaders always need a relentless focus on creating a competitive strategy and providing strategic direction and alignment. When this is augmented by a Continuous Improvement culture, leadership must nourish and sustain it. Achieving this requires delivering a very high quality and quantity of key leadership skills and techniques selected by Pareto analysis. It also requires rigorous prioritizing mechanisms to decide which of the resultant avalanche of employee suggestions to focus resources on. Organizations also need to plan for how they will ride the tidal wave of previously invisible talent unleashed when artificial barriers are systematically removed (see Chapter 12).

---

* For the wider dangers of the lack of cognitive diversity see Syed 2020.

The key lessons for senior leaders are to ensure that your leadership approach is designed using design criteria similar to those detailed earlier and that it systematically leverages a powerful form of employee engagement such as RME. In addition, it must systematically leverage Continuous Improvement capability spread widely and deeply across your organization and not confined to specific functions and job roles.

Interviewed for this book, Bacardi's Cain Ashworth, supply chain director Western Europe, said, "This leadership approach gave me the foundation for my entire career, how to build high-performance teams, how to have the right conversations, how to recruit the right capabilities." In the next chapter we will see that even with the best employee engagement and enablement, the best Continuous Improvement approach, and the best leadership development system, leaders also must powerfully signal their commitment to culture change.

Signaling Commitment

*A revolutionary way of reacting to each other that
will be long remembered as transformative.*

John Keogh
Quality director, Seagate Technology

John Keogh's use of the word "revolutionary" in the quote above is significant; RME is not for those who are playing at culture change. RME tests leaders' commitment and humility. It is not suitable for organizations that are "fat and happy."

The Importance of Addressing Employee Skepticism

When RME starts, employees look for signs of the commitment from their senior leaders. In the initial All Employee Workshops, they frequently ask questions about sincerity. They are testing if we are simply giving them permission to speak out: "Is this only lip service?" or less polite versions of the same sentiment are commonly expressed. Leaders must demonstrate without doubt that they are not passionate in style only. Employees wonder "if these guys are for real" and "what will happen when the heat comes on?"

Employees are rightly skeptical about whether their leaders will really listen and act. They hear the RME vision, but wonder if their leaders will really revolutionize HR processes if the data shows this is needed to drive the pace of change. Employees question if their leaders are comfortable with what I call maximizing solution space. Will leaders really make joint decisions on Consensus Day and then implement all of them in full?

Frequently this skepticism is expressed significantly less constructively, but the skepticism itself is a healthy input to the overall process; it drives better outcomes as ideas are developed and tested scientifically rather than hierarchically.

RME is a process, one that cannot achieve its potential without the leadership of individuals at all levels. The outcomes associated with RME would not have been possible without individuals responding to skepticism by demonstrating integrity and that "things are different now."

This demonstration of commitment is not confined to RME. For example, the Tata Group began its lean journey by fixing its employees' roofs before applying Continuous Improvement to its factories.* When Tata chose to prioritize the improvement of the leaking roofs of its employees over the profitability of its factories, employees noticed; Tata's commitment to its founding values and its integrity was demonstrated in action not just in words.

Signaling Commitment: Examples

Let's see how other courageous people have signaled commitment to the culture change that they created and owned.

---

* See Tata Group Publications 2008.

"I Could Not Take the Promotion"

In one RME, the site director was promoted to a senior corporate role. This reflected his site outperforming all other locations across the world. His successor was selected via a process in which corporate talent development was the predominant criterion. This succession process gave little weight to truly understanding what was required to continue the momentum that had doubled output on the site rapidly.

When the site director learned who his successor was to be, he engaged him on the culture of the site and how it was created by employees and the multiple ways in which it was sustained. These efforts were futile. The successor would have been the only person on site not to understand the culture underpinning all the performance metrics. This would have been deeply disrespectful to a workforce trained and willing to challenge upward to sustain their culture.

As the site director told me, "I could not leave the people who have created all this to be undermined in this way; I could not take the promotion."

In corporate life this was a gutsy thing to do, and his corporate leaders were humble enough to leave him in position and include him in any future discussions on who his successor should be.*The site director's values and commitment to the team he had built and nurtured outweighed the financial and career hits. The employees on the site are not aware of this sacrifice, but he has signaled his commitment to his bosses, and in so many other ways locally, that they know leadership commitment is not an issue.

---

* There is a wider issue concerning the underappreciation of operations and science in organizations. A key lesson is that operational sites should be led by leaders who understand high-performance Continuous Improvement cultures among large employee groups and what it takes to build and sustain them. These sites are too important to be used as "broadening opportunities" for talented leaders lacking in these competencies. Succession planning, yes, but damaging competitiveness and creating employee cynicism about leadership, no.

"We Will Find a Way"

Let's consider the crucial issue of span of control. When span of control is too large, frontline leaders lack the time to adequately interact with their teams; employees experience this as lack of respect. During the initial RME workshops, employees report major delays in getting responses to questions and suggestions and often attribute negative intent to their leaders; this in turn fosters a feeling of "them versus us." Boston Scientific's Consensus Day in 2015 featured employee representative after employee representative outlining many symptoms of frontline leaders having too large a span of control.

Having listened to multiple examples, I invited the group to move to root cause identification. This included the group calculating how many queries a frontline leader would receive in an average shift, given the span of control. The group quickly realized the site had accidentally set the frontline leaders up for failure with an impossible workload in which something had to give.

Employee representatives noted that the scope for RME included no increase in cost. Any solutions that reduced span of control would mean an increase in headcount for which there was no budget. Signaling of commitment was needed at this point, and the Boston senior team rose to the challenge. Operations director James Lyons intervened to say that although there was nothing in this year's budget, they had time to address this. It would take time to restructure thoroughly as it would involve piloting the new approach; by then this new priority could be addressed in subsequent budgets. Other senior leaders voiced their agreement. Their sentiment was "we will find a way," that budget issues should not prevent ensuring that frontline leaders were set up for success. This was a seminal point in that Consensus Day; senior leaders, previously quiet and in listening mode, stepped in when needed to remove a financial obstacle in the way of solving a major "them versus us" issue for employees.

Once that limiting assumption around budget was removed, the group energetically debated and agreed upon the actions that established a "Setting the Production Team Up for Success" workstream.

This in turn led to the introduction of the line facilitator role in Boston Scientific, which reduced span of control and delivered multiple other benefits such as freeing up managers for longer-term improvements, reducing the "step-up" required from the shop floor into management positions and turbocharging response times to all stakeholders including employees. The introduction of this role was subsequently found to have a surprisingly short payback time for some. The payback was measured by tangible increases in productivity and quality. More difficult to measure were the additional and cumulative effects of a workforce with frontline leaders and a wider technical team with the time to have the quality and quantity of conversations crucial to success.

Something similar happened in Outokumpu's Consensus Day in 2002 when Olof Faxander, the site general manager, and his team similarly removed the limiting assumptions around budget. These scope limitations are necessary in the earlier stages of RME when the transition to adult-adult dialogue has to be achieved by the facilitator. Without those limitations it is very easy for some employees to adopt an unrealistic child-parent "we want everything and we want it now" mindset that is not conducive to data-based diagnostic work and, if indulged, reduces innovation and sets unrealistic expectations. In Outokumpu's case, the initial scope limitations were necessary to transition to that scientific adult-adult mindset but, once that was established, became an obstacle to progress on Consensus Day when the site's dilapidated equipment needed to be restored to competitiveness. In such circumstances it was crucial to innovate around them.*

---

* It is common for nationalized industries, and ex nationalized industries, to suffer from prolonged lack of capital investment and maintenance. In the public sector, they compete with hospitals, schools, and the like for finite resources; in addition, it is electorally easier for politicians to starve long-term capital investment in favor of more electorally popular current expenditure on wages, subsidies, and so on.

"We Have to Get to the Night Shift Tonight"

The Consensus Day in Textron in 2001 started at 8:30 a.m. and concluded at 12:30 p.m. the next day—16 hours. It was held in an off-site hotel some distance from the site. Part of the Consensus Day process is immediate feedback to employees. This ensures that employees learn the outcomes of Consensus Day directly from other employees, not via the usual managerial channels.

Consensus Day had agreed on the format and common language for the feedback and had decided which employee representatives were briefing which specific groups back on site. When the Joint Change Plan was drafted and displayed, employees mentioned that, as it was Thursday, the night shift would be leaving at 6 a.m. and would not be back on-site until Sunday. Realizing that this was an unacceptable time lag, the team chosen to brief the nightshift jumped into a car, drove to the site, and conducted the night shift briefing. It was 3 a.m. before they went home.

They had already worked a 16-hour day and they were tired, but they knew that the night shift could not be an afterthought, briefed on Sunday night when everyone else was briefed on Friday. They did the right thing, not the easy thing.

Publicly Display of Uncensored Feedback

Sue Savage led Rolls-Royce Experimental Logistics in 2007. A key obstacle to successful culture change is the belief that management will not "change its spots."

The Experimental Logistics Consensus Day had decided to measure progress against the management capability aspect of its Joint Change Plan by developing an upward feedback process for all managers. This included how the new Behavioral Standards were working in practice. This was separate from the top-down corporate survey, which employees felt was too generic to track progress specifically against the Consensus Day outcomes. RME explicitly encourages an environment in which feedback is seen as positive. Sue displayed the employee feedback on how she was modeling and referencing the Behavioral Standards, verbatim and in full, publicly on the walls of her buildings. She referred to it as she walked around talking to her teams. Sue ensured that the uncomplimentary comments were not censored but were there for everyone to see.

Talking about feedback as a gift is cheap; displaying your personal feedback signaled commitment. Sue's openness and nondefensive attitude to feedback was later formally noted by employees. In Rolls-Royce's official engagement survey that followed, the group soared from near the bottom to 4 to 14 percent above corporate average in scores for key metrics important to employees, such as local leadership and leading by example.

100 Percent Attendance and Public Apology

In 2003, Coca-Cola's Edmonton plant was one of the lowest performing sites in the network with adversarial industrial relations despite high pay and good conditions. When Richard Davies was appointed as general manager, he had to address this quickly. In the last 20 minutes of RME's initial employee workshops, senior leaders join to listen and understand what employees are diagnosing as the major obstacles to success.

Richard ensured he attended the end of every workshop; he heard employee testimony about worrying events, including intimidation previously unknown to senior management. After a few workshops he felt compelled to act. He replied to the forceful feedback by saying:

> I am responsible for this site. Hearing these examples make me ashamed. I apologize to every employee who has experienced this. I can't change the past, but I can work with you to agree a change plan and new culture to prevent it ever happening again. That is what Consensus Day is for and I can't wait to get these issues resolved, I just need you to work with me to achieve that.

With the leadership of Richard and his team, supplemented with a talented group of internal facilitators representing all areas of the location, the RME Joint Change Plan was implemented. Within a year it was the highest performing location in the Coca-Cola network, and it soon began to win national manufacturing excellence awards such as the Cranfield School of Business FMCG Factory of the Year.

"Equality" for Pay Cuts?

In the private sector, when recession happens survival is an issue. Often job and pay cuts are implemented to prevent insolvency. Organizations frequently impose across-the-board pay reductions at the same percentage, claiming this is fair.

Directski was a small startup when the 2008–2010 Recession struck. Its RME process happened against this background. As unemployment increased, the market for ski holidays collapsed. Pay had to be cut, but not in the so-called fair way of many organizations. As managing director, Anthony Collins cut his own pay by 20 percent, while his senior team took a 15 percent pay cut. On that basis he went to his employees and asked for a 10 percent pay cut, committing to a full reinstatement of pay levels as soon as conditions improved. The pay cuts for staff were reversed first. Later, as business recovered further, the senior team's pay cut was also reversed.

Managing Interference

Steve Long ran GKN's factory in Luton. He attended a workshop where I outlined the CHPM approach to leadership. After that experience he volunteered his site to test the use of the CHPM in GKN's global lean program and trained all his leaders in the content.

Steve opened the local workshops by asking every manager to tell him of any event or interaction that could distract from 100 percent focus on the content. He then arranged for someone else, often himself, to take responsibility for handling that interference. His message was: "Every part of this matters and, with my support, I expect to see it implemented 100 percent; it is not like your previous experiences of leadership training."

He followed through on his signaling by checking in with his leaders about how they were doing implementing the skills and techniques and he modeled, and he referenced the content and philosophy every day; it was not possible to doubt his commitment. I recommend his example to every leader wishing to signal commitment.

Summary

"Culture is tested every day" is a theme of this book. The people referred to above are a distinguished sample of the many brave people who signal their commitment when it matters most. RME cannot succeed without their humility, passion, and sheer dedication. I am honored to work with them and see what they achieve for their organizations, their sites, their families, and their communities.

Great cultures, if not sustained, will deteriorate. In the following chapter, we will learn how to prevent this from happening.

CHAPTER 9

Rapid Yes—
but Sustainable?

The engagement and enablement are deep and
change attitudes rapidly, but to sustain this powerful
initial momentum requires systematic leadership.

John Keogh
Quality director, Seagate Technology

In the quote above, John Keogh was discussing the role of leadership in sustaining the initial improvements made in the early stages of RME. Many other leaders have discussed this point; they have wondered if RME is rapid but unsustainable—is it like a rocket that flies to the sky but then falls to earth quickly also? Even if we sustain in the initial years, as the culture's creators become a smaller and smaller percentage of the workforce, how do we sustain longer term?

RME's vision argues for creating a high-performance culture so deeply owned by employees that it sustains itself regardless of changes in senior leadership. Is that vision possible? Or is the maximum we can achieve successive approximations toward it?

Let's start examining these questions by approaching the challenge in the shoes of an employee experiencing RME. Imagine you are that employee. You are surprised when you are given power to make decisions that determine the future of your workplace. Then you witness changes happening that were widely proclaimed to be impossible. Later, you see investment levels increase. Your belief in what is possible grows as new jobs are advertised and policies change that create opportunities for people like you, opportunities you had previously regarded as out of reach, such as becoming a manager or technical specialist or group facilitator. You notice that the peer group influence of cynical voices diminishes as the latter's confident and loud predictions are demonstrated to be wrong. As the full CHPM is implemented well, those cynical voices either become more open-minded or find themselves being cynical somewhere else—ideally working for one of your competitors!*

The challenge is how to maintain this rate of improvement as the new culture matures. New employees experience the culture and adopt it, but it is not theirs in the same sense or at the same level of intensity; they inherit it rather than create it themselves. Let's look at some examples.

Doubling the size of the DePuy Synthes workforce resulted in most managers becoming inheritors of the culture rather than its creators. This is a major challenge for every implementation of RME. Alan Heneghan's experience of joining Boston Scientific, six years after RME, showed that initial success can been sustained (see Chapter 6). The challenge is to sustain the culture for longer than six years, especially in situations like Boston and DePuy where the sheer size of the job expansion leads to the opening of an entirely new second site with a potentially new culture of its own.

What can we do to mitigate this? How do we maintain the passionate support for the culture as key people are promoted off-site, are headhunted by other organizations, become consultants, retire,

---

* Figure 9.6 will show how to ensure that timidity around accountability and risk aversion do not prevent you gaining the full team dynamics benefits of using the CHPM.

and are replaced by new starters? Let's look for answers by understanding the sustainability role of the three key focus areas of the book (Figure 9.1).

FIGURE 9.1 **Three Sustainability Focus Areas**

Let's now look at how each of the three overlapping and leveraged focus areas help sustain the culture, starting with the engagement process.

Ensure Authenticity of the Engagement Process

The culture has little chance of sustaining if the employees who created it do not testify to the authenticity of RME. New starters need to hear widespread testimony such as:

- "It did happen; I was there."

- "I was like you; I did not believe it was possible, but that is exactly how the Behavioral Standards were created."
- "The reason you can change shifts to suit your family and save so much in childcare costs is because we prioritized the issue and Consensus Day changed the policy* . . . it didn't just happen by itself!"

When new starters hear this testimony, they begin to understand how different and emotionally significant it is to have the workplace culture created and owned by employees rather than implemented by management on employees, a key differentiator of RME. New starters were not there at the time, they did not experience the roller coaster of emotions, but clearly something big and unusual happened. This creates curiosity that, we will see in Chapter 11, plays a key part in driving receptivity to new ideas, to Continuous Improvement, and to innovation.

Symbolism is also important. When new employees realize that the facilitators running their induction to the organization's culture are not managers or HR staff but frontline employees, this sends multiple messages about hierarchy, respect for individuals, and leadership style. This in turn creates more curiosity.

When employee facilitators run new starter workshops, they report enthusiastic comments on how different the culture is from where the new starters previously worked. This happens even when, as Alan Heneghan mentioned earlier (Chapter 6), they have come from successful organizations with good cultures. This enthuses those facilitators and creates a virtuous circle that helps sustain progress.

Some new starters inquire further and discover how RME "happened"; they are amazed to learn that on Consensus Day employees outnumbered managers by more than two to one, that the only group who did not have the right to nominate agenda items for

---

* In this RME, comparing post-tax income and childcare costs revealed that some employees had previously used approximately a third of their post-tax income on childcare costs.

Consensus Day were the senior team, and that all decisions were publicly displayed on the walls and photographed to prevent any note-taking bias or distortions in the recording process. When new starters learn how the Behavioral Standards were created, they see that the subgroup that transformed all the behavioral data into a set of Behavioral Standards was elected by the Consensus Day group and had a large employee majority. This increases the sense that they have joined somewhere with a special approach to employees.

Later, the use of direct quotes from employees during the RME initial workshops in the subsequent training adds to this authenticity. Facilitators use an exercise whereby employees plot what they said in their original workshops on a map of the Behavioral Standards. This leads to gleeful shouts of "I said that!" thus adding to both ownership and authenticity—and fun!

These examples enable employees to reassure new starters that the site culture was truly created by employees. As Alan Heneghan said, "By God, I could really feel it, instantly."

Authenticity is also key to how improvement techniques are introduced. Let's see how this "pull for improvement" is created, how authenticity grows as employees look for ways to improve their work. Figure 9.2 depicts how this happens.

Sustaining via Continuous Improvement

Let's start by examining how RME strengthens the Continuous Improvement and quality processes and helps sustain them. Once we have done that, we will consider the reciprocal sustaining effects. Martin O'Riordan, director, value chain leader Janssen Pharmaceutical Companies, reflected on RME's contribution to winning the Shingo Prize:

> The transformation in culture driven by the rapid mass engagement was the foundation and enabler for the site's successful lean journey, which culminated in a Gold Shingo

FIGURE 9.2 The Role of Authenticity in Creating Pull for Continuous Improvement

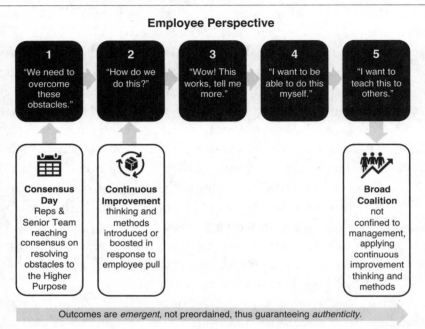

Employee Perspective

1	2	3	4	5
"We need to overcome these obstacles."	"How do we do this?"	"Wow! This works, tell me more."	"I want to be able to do this myself."	"I want to teach this to others."

Consensus Day
Reps & Senior Team reaching consensus on resolving obstacles to the Higher Purpose

Continuous Improvement
thinking and methods introduced or boosted in response to employee pull

Broad Coalition
not confined to management, applying continuous improvement thinking and methods

Outcomes are *emergent*, not preordained, thus guaranteeing *authenticity*.

Prize—the benchmark for Operational Excellence. The site's metrics tell the success story. This intervention was a game changer that is still clearly evident six years later.

The Shingo assessors saw the impact of tens of thousands of *informal* improvement-oriented conversations cumulatively leveraging the formal Continuous Improvement activities on the site. These informal inputs are individually inaccessible to external assessors but cumulatively critical to the quality of the formal processes. In Chapter 7 we saw the pivotal impact of coaching as a daily informal spontaneous capability; the full application of the CHPM multiplied that leverage via the systematic increase in both the quality and quantity of the other key leadership interventions.

Paul Kearney reflected on how the level of engagement created by RME impacted Boston Scientific's already strong quality system:

> There was a powerful effect on the Quality System: at the front end, the level of employee engagement in quality investigations increased dramatically, trust in management's intent had been created. Similarly, at the back end, implementation changed from employees seeing it as "they are doing this to me and my process" to "we are doing this together to make this better." In addition, the Behavioral Standards created an expectation that conversations would be constructive and nonjudgmental which disarmed fear and removed negative assumptions.

Why does the impact of RME on Continuous Improvement and on the related quality system illustrated reinforce the culture created by RME? Let's remember a key visual from earlier (Figure 9.3).

When a competitive Continuous Improvement capability is created, it acts as a major bulwark against the erosion of the new culture. Key to successful Continuous Improvement is sustaining the gains made via the day-to-day alignment of leadership actions, habits, and processes. Many experts and senior leaders have noticed the correlation between successful Continuous Improvement implementation and RME.* John Bicheno, founding director of the Lean Enterprise Research Council MSc at Cardiff University, observed: "Everywhere I see this approach, I see systematic and sustained engagement in improvement." The RME Behavioral Standards are often seen simply as the codification of the new culture, but they are also designed to sustain that new culture, to be inherently self-sustaining.

---

* Many RME implementations happened because of frustration with the level of employee engagement with Continuous Improvement.

FIGURE 9.3 Leverage Effects Within RME

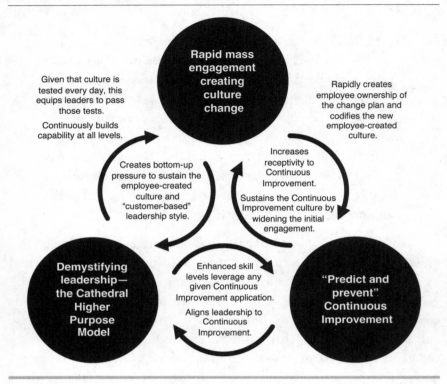

Designing Sustainability into the Behavioral Standards

When first exposed to RME, it is usual for employees to be very skeptical that a new employee-owned culture will be sustained. Typical comments include:

- "If managers talk the talk but don't walk the walk, what can we do?"
- "There are people who will not want to change their behavior, and when they are seen to get away with it, others will follow, and it will collapse."

- "How do we stop this going off track when people act inconsistently with our new approach?"

These are valid concerns and contribute to the perceived failure of many attempts at culture change. Relevant here is a quote attributed to the Irish political philosopher Edmund Burke: "All that is necessary for evil to succeed is that good men do nothing."

How does Burke's principle help us sustain a new culture? He challenged the traditional Christian belief of "turning the other cheek." He argued it is not enough to lead by example alone; we need to proactively challenge anything that is wrong. When I train the Consensus Day Behavioral Standards subgroup, I remind them of Burke's point and emphasize that if we are serious about creating something worthwhile, we need to fight for it and prevent others from undermining it.

Many people shy away from challenging negative behaviors; this is at best, well-meaning positivity bias. We feel more comfortable being positive, and it is easy to assume that dealing with negative behaviors is somehow negative and to be avoided. How many adult problem behaviors have you seen simply go away without the uncomfortable conversations necessary to address them? What can be more positive than eliminating behaviors such as talking negatively behind others' backs referred to by Paul Deasy earlier (Chapter 6)? Such behaviors undermine the new culture and need to be challenged, respectfully challenged, but challenged in the spirit of positive intent outlined in Chapter 6. As the facilitator guide for one Behavioral Standards workshop says: "Remember these Standards do not classify people who get it wrong as 'bad people.'"

The spirit of our challenge is that when an individual breaches one of our Behavioral Standards, it is a case of "a good person who made a mistake" not a "bad person." That is why the RME Behavioral Standards are designed to include one that sustains the other standards. It does this by empowering employees to challenge anyone who breaches them—no matter how senior.

In Chapter 1, when the recently promoted frontline leader challenged his new director, he pointed to that Behavioral Standard on the wall to affirm the cultural expectation to do so. He trembled inside, but his culture empowered him to act, and he defended his culture despite the career risk. Culture is sustained by the courageous challenges of those prepared to fight for it when it is being undermined.

Would he and his colleagues have done this without a Behavioral Standard specifically empowering them to do so? Who knows, it is a counterfactual, but it certainly helped to have the right, indeed the obligation, to do so visible on the wall for them to point to as the site's policy.

So far, we have seen that sustainability is enhanced by the authenticity of the original engagement process, by the two-way leverage with Continuous Improvement, and by the structural design of the Behavioral Standards. What role does leadership play in sustainability?

Designing Sustainability into the Leadership System

Rather than looking at sustaining in the abstract, it is worthwhile reminding ourselves about what we are sustaining. Deirdre Cooney, Amgen's leader, operational excellence, Dun Laoghaire, provided a key focus when she said: "Lots of people talk about the Toyota principle of Respect for People but confuse it with politeness; this leadership approach, particularly its distinctive Double-Diamond coaching, delivers it in practice."

Any dilution in the fundamental feeling that all employees are treated with respect, that their feelings and ideas matter, will quickly undermine the culture. Turnover in leadership positions is usually higher than in non-leadership jobs. If there is high leadership turnover, within a few years of starting RME, we can find that more leaders have not directly experienced the emotional power of the founding process than those who did.

Failing to manage these transition issues leads to good cultures ossifying and then declining. Hence the criticality of managing succession planning at all levels (see Chapter 12). The CHPM addresses this issue by including numerous sustaining mechanisms that apply equally to leaders who were part of the founding process and those joining from outside (Figure 9.4).

FIGURE 9.4 **The Cathedral Higher Purpose Model**

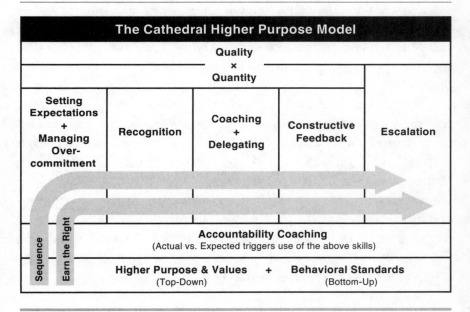

How is sustainability designed into the implementation of the CHPM? Accountability Coaching systematically reinforces and sustains all skill levels and standards (including Behavioral Standards) within an organization. To have credibility when Accountability Coaching, leaders must master the entire model.*

All leaders at all levels and all facilitators are trained to model the behaviors and skill levels required. They are also trained to

---

* The quality of skill level is crucial for success; doing the unsexy repetitive effort necessary to make daily marginal gains is underrepresented in many leadership programs.

reference, that is, "join the dots" between the original RME, the origins and meaning of the Behavioral Standards, and how the integrated series of linkages between engagement, enablement, leadership, and Continuous Improvement operate in practice.*

All leaders and facilitators are also trained to use curiosity, stories, vivid language, process confirmation via fun quizzes, and humor to make learning memorable and thus accessible to the brain when needed (see Chapter 11). As it is difficult to sustain anything you can't remember, this aids sustainability. Their training includes specific sustaining mechanisms in each of the six one-day CHPM phases.

Transferring training from external trainers to a constantly refreshed team of internal facilitators (including senior team members) ensures those lured away by other organizations are replaced by people who joined after RME but are determined to sustain and improve what they have experienced.

These facilitators are selected to ensure all functions, groups, and shifts are represented. This guarantees that there is always a facilitator close by to help employees use their Behavioral Standards day-to-day in their work and to overcome their challenges. The sustaining effect is thus guaranteed to cover all areas and shifts.

The Sustainability Role of the Internal Facilitation Teams

An important goal of RME is to reach client independence as soon as possible. There are two types of internal facilitator within RME, namely the facilitator of the Behavioral Standards and the facilitator of the six-day, six-phase CHPM program that supports RME.

After Consensus Day, facilitators are selected to train everyone in the Behavioral Standards. Facilitators are selected based on

---

* I recommend that the original visual of the RME process used in the employee workshops remains in training rooms permanently so that facilitators can walk over and make these links explicit.

capability to facilitate and peer group credibility—not position in the hierarchy or competence in delivering presentations.* Shop floor and junior employees training directors is a happy and symbolic outcome of this approach. Imagine the cultural message a new director receives when a junior employee skillfully facilitates discussion on the meaning of the site's culture.

The internal facilitators who deliver the leadership training have already been trained in the CHPM and have excelled in modeling and referencing its skills and techniques. Both groups of facilitators include at least one senior team member to act as an empathetic link between the facilitator teams and the senior team and to manage interference. In these multiple and reinforcing ways, the CHPM sustains both the new culture and the continuously improving skill levels necessary to overcome future challenges.

The Sustaining Architecture

Armed with clear and mutually reinforcing role clarity, both groups of facilitators forge and sustain the new culture (see Figure 9.4). They act as informal cultural influencers active in all functions and present on all shifts and locations. Figure 9.5 illustrates the cumulative impact of all these sustaining mechanisms. With this architecture in place the organization has created multiple reinforcing sustaining mechanisms.

Even with this sustaining architecture a danger develops around managing team dynamics as the culture evolves. Let's see how to avoid this danger.

---

* A common error is to assume good presenters make good facilitators: some do, but some don't; the skill set is different, and in some respects opposite.

FIGURE 9.5 The Sustaining Architecture

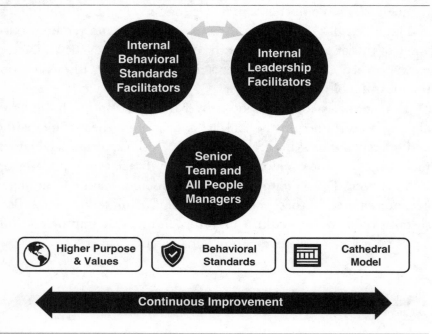

The Sustaining Role of Managing Team Dynamics

We saw in Chapter 7 how leadership interventions become necessarily more forceful as a leader moves rightward in the CHPM. Timing movement rightward is crucial, and two opposite mistakes can undermine the new culture. This is visualized in Figure 9.6.

The twin errors are, in the early stages, being too impatient with employees failing to adopt the new standards and, in the longer term, being too tolerant for too long when the new culture is widely adopted among employees. The first error gives the impression that RME is a disguised "management crackdown" and thus undermines its Higher Purpose; the second error undermines the new culture by tolerating breaches of it. The latter implies your culture is optional

FIGURE 9.6 **Sustaining High Performance via Managing Team Dynamics**

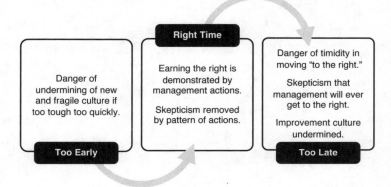

and is highly demotivating for its most able advocates and highest performers. The team dynamics awareness and skills necessary to avoid either error are covered in Phase 1 of the CHPM program.

Having looked at how RME's initial mass engagement, Behavioral Standards, leadership, Continuous Improvement approach, and facilitation teams all sustain the new culture . . . what could possibly go wrong?

Let's look at when and how things suboptimize and what we can learn from those experiences in the next chapter. In that way we can predict and prevent this happening in your organization.

When RME Has Suboptimized

*We were promoted too soon into senior corporate roles;
we were moved away from what had been achieved;
it was right for our careers and our bank balances
but so wrong for the business and our employees.*

Mike Moran
HR director, Rolls-Royce Civil Aerospace

When preparing this chapter, I encountered a problem. Interviewing a minority of leaders involved, there was pushback to discussing "what might have been": they were happy with their RME results. They had made significant improvements. I was told: "Yes, it could have been even better, but we did some great things, we just didn't do as well as some others."

Leaders can only achieve as much as is possible in the circumstances. Leaders are not dictators; they have stakeholders, and key functional specialists often report outside the site. Matrix organizations and external reporting complicates the rigorous accountability central to RME—even for the most skilled leaders.

How Mass Production and Short-Term Thinking Killed Lean at the Expense of Customers

In a pub on a cold winter's night in 2021 the ex–plant manager's passion lit up the gloom; he was proud of what had been achieved and angry at seeing it undermined by what he described as lack of leadership in high places. He summed it up by saying, "They couldn't turn the lights off on their expensive white elephant, so they turned our lights off."

I have seen what happened to his site twice in very different sectors. In both situations, the technical breakthroughs achieved by implementing Consensus Day's Joint Change Plan threatened the corporate strategy, unknown to local management, to concentrate production in a massive new factory. Such mega plants are often justified by claimed economies of scale. To gain agreement for the capital investment, these calculations tend to be extremely optimistic.* To realize the benefits promised by the sponsors, such large factories must be fed by very high volumes. Unless organizations either gain market share, increase the size of the market, or both, feeding the monster plant reduces the products allocated to existing factories.

In one RME, the industry status quo was that customers had to wait for months before receiving their orders. One of the post–Consensus Day technical breakthroughs enabled customers to have their delivery within a week of placing their order. Providing product to the market so much quicker would have transformed customers' own businesses as they could supply in a much more agile manner—in smaller quantities far more often—reflecting the

---

* A cause of many public investments running widely over budget.

actual demand pattern of their own customers. This in turn would significantly reduce cost across the entire supply chain as the cost and quality issues associated with storing, counting, and then moving inventory were minimized.

This was a huge opportunity to leverage this technical breakthrough in every plant, delighting customers and immediately increasing market share. After a lag, the market would have expanded as what was previously seen as impossible became commercially feasible. In addition, this would have increased jobs, shortened supply chains, and made multiple customers more competitive throughout interlocking supply chains. The opportunity was not taken. Instead, a corporate decision was made to close the breakthrough facility and transfer production to the new mega plant, thereby ignoring the transformational opportunities. It was easier, less potentially career-threatening, to remove the embarrassment of an old plant outperforming the shiny and new investment than to give customers a level of service they had never experienced and were therefore not explicitly asking for.

This happened in both cases. It is a tragic example of the market transformation opportunities possible with lean manufacturing being overpowered by a toxic combination of mass production models still dominant in HQ, zero-sum thinking (assuming market size is a given), and sunk cost affecting decision-making. It is difficult for some senior leaders to admit mistakes, especially when it involves multimillion-dollar investments.

Clearly there are corporate strategy and leadership issues here,* but the real tragedy was the loss of opportunity to transform both markets and the loss of jobs. Such examples also reinforce both management and employee cynicism and make it even more difficult for innovative leaders to convince their workforces of their sincerity.

RME is usually local in nature, a form of powerful differentiation. It respects and builds on the culture and history of the site.

---

* Hence the need for Chapter 7.

This is key to the face validity or immediate credibility so crucial when trust is being earned. As such, given organizational hierarchy, it is always vulnerable to decisions made higher in the hierarchy by senior leaders who fail to grasp the value of what has been created by their local team.

To conclude where we began, the plant manager quoted at the start of this chapter went on to say:

> Before Consensus Day, I asked the corporate CEO if we were able to deliver such a revolutionary improvement in service and cost reduction to our customers, would it keep our plant open. He looked me in the eye and guaranteed it would. To be fair to them, I don't think they believed how much we would achieve so quickly. When we delivered even more, they opened their monster plant and still shut us. The new plant had too many reputations on the line, and we, and the wider supply chain, were collateral damage. I try not to think about how many jobs in the wider supply chain would have been saved and created if we had deployed what we had learned.

Lessons for Corporate Decision Makers

A key lesson for corporate decision makers is to appreciate what your local team has created before making "improvements." One plant manager looking back at the decline of performance after a change in site and corporate leadership was frustrated that the new leadership made little effort to understand how this site's culture and high performance had been created or to investigate what was necessary to sustain it.

He described the new leadership being "blown away by the engagement of the workforce" but taking it for granted rather than cherishing it. The new leadership actually reduced the solution-space of operational managers. In addition too many senior people lacked the courage to push back, looking to safeguard their short-term career prospects rather than what they had seen transform the business.

In this example, the short-term benefit of focusing just on cost rather than value and culture soon evaporated, to the surprise of the new leadership who did not understand what they had done. The plant manager sadly explained that "a lot of great guys became disillusioned and left and the cynics got the evidence they needed thus worsening the situation further."

For readers involved in allocating capital investment, these examples highlight the danger of underestimating the value that customers attach to an outstanding and responsive service and a short, agile, and reliable supply chain. In one of the examples above customers soon voted with their wallet: they much preferred the global best OTIF (on time in full), highest quality and dispatch on demand service offered by the RME site to the much slower and less flexible supply the replacement mega plant delivered.

Finally, a key method of avoiding suboptimization is to maximize the cultural impact of site visits. If you are a corporate leader, how you conduct local site visits is an opportunity to model and reference a high-performance culture. For example, when reviewing an issue, avoid assuming that the main cause of failure is local; instead ask: "What are we doing in corporate to make this more difficult for you?" (See "Managing on Green" in Chapter 7.) Use that feedback to improve the interaction, systematically and with humility, between HQ and the locations.

When you have gathered similar feedback from multiple locations, it is crucial to include those site-based employees who provided the feedback in the emergent corporate improvement activities. They will passionately help to test tentative diagnoses and to inexpensively trial possible solutions across multiple locations, thus replicating the approach that created RME.

Finally, maximize recognition by giving the local providers of the original feedback key roles in both the communication of these improvement projects globally and when presenting the new processes that emerge from them locally and globally. If you do all these things, you can turn "I'm here from HQ to help" from a perceived threat to a genuine reflection of the experiences of those working closest to customers and suppliers.

Lack of Leadership Stability

In Chapter 1 we saw how frequent changes in senior leadership create employee cynicism. The senior team Diagnostic Day explores any expected changes in senior leadership and the negative effect this is likely to have if implemented before the new culture has become established. In one RME, the most senior person informed me, just before Consensus Day, that she had been headhunted for another job and would announce her departure in the weeks following Consensus Day. When she did so, this simultaneously boosted the peer credibility of those who had predicted lack of leadership commitment and undermined the credibility of the most positive employees. This was compounded by the decision to rely on existing leadership training, the same training that had failed to address the issues previously! An excellent group of internal facilitators, who had experienced the effectiveness of the RME training approach, felt unsupported by the continuation of the leadership issues identified in the employee workshops. Progress stalled within a year.

Unintended Consequences of Conventional HR Practice

One of the many advantages of integrating Continuous Improvement philosophy with employee engagement is that long-term thinking is systematically reinforced (see Liker 2004, Principle 1). How organizations see leadership career planning is key here.

In RME, it is crucial to avoid the misguided but well-intentioned promotion of key individuals after the initial major achievements— the rapid part of RME—but before the new culture can sustain itself. Cultures are initially fragile but grow, action by action, over time; even with the power and pace of RME, the new culture is on trial in the eyes of employees, and it is tested every day. In the quote that opened the chapter, Rolls-Royce's Mike Moran reflected on the unintended consequences of his own promotion soon after RME had delivered major changes but when the culture was still fragile:

> We were promoted too soon into senior corporate roles; we were moved away from what had been achieved; it was right for our careers and our bank balances but so wrong for the business and our employees.

If you dilute the team of people most passionate about the new culture, the people most effective at modeling and referencing the RME philosophy and leadership models (see Chapter 7), you weaken your new culture while it is still fragile.

This has policy implications as it challenges how promotions are earned; it is crucial that sustained results, not superficially impressive early progress, are the basis for promotion and that this expectation is clearly communicated when employing and promoting leaders. This challenges organizations to rethink how we reward our leaders and to value staying in position for long enough to demonstrate sustained improvement. In other words, we need to avoid feeding a "fear of missing out" (FOMO) among our leaders. We need our leaders to keep their eyes on the ball, not dream about the next game, to stay in position longer than has become fashionable in the West. We must stop punishing leaders' careers for doing the right things for their employees, departments, and sites. Our reward systems must prevent our leaders feeling their careers are stalled. Finally, we must educate the external jobs market despite its vested interest in encouraging the rapid promotion groupthink. Even when we ensure the initial stability of leadership and we change expectations around the basis and speed of promotion, this philosophy of what counts as success must be maintained through successive changes in senior leadership.

Succession Planning

One RME site was very successful for many years after but had recently stalled. I interviewed several senior leaders who had worked at the site. One said, "In recent years, a succession of new senior leaders was appointed without an understanding of what we had created with our employees; they wanted to put their own stamp on things; the ownership of the employees sustained but the new senior leaders did not recognize the significance and power of what they had inherited."

A shop floor employee on the same site confirmed this analysis, saying, "It is sad after what had been achieved in the first seven or eight years; we are still better than we were before and we are operationally successful but we have lost the pace and passion for improvement that our culture created; I think we could get that back, but management don't understand why we were so successful and this has strengthened cynicism and anti-management feelings which we worked so hard to overcome."

Dilution and Deprioritization by Well-Intentioned Management Additions

Sometimes well-meaning interventions can be counterproductive and dilutive. Ann Bentley, global board director for Rider Levett Bucknall, gave an example: "Our Behavioral Standards gave us a willingness to challenge in all directions to improve the business contributing to massive growth, especially in the early years. Over 18 years, as senior management changed, we added different initiatives causing confusion and weakening the focus and accountability we had created. Our good intentions diluted the impact, and we filtered the original power of the process. This led to selective implementation."

What can we learn from these examples? I aim for clients to become independent with their own internal facilitators and other sustaining mechanisms, but dialogue with other organizations attempting RME is also crucial. I encourage this by introductions and best practice sharing among my clients. This helps avoid predictable, albeit well-meaning mistakes such as those outlined above.

Nonclients make a different mistake when they copy without a deep enough understanding. They often dilute the prioritizing strength of the CHPM. This has happened when organizations have attempted to simply copy it without fully understanding the systems effects of the full process. I have attended conferences and workshops where speakers have confidently presented my CHPM while displaying a lack of depth and nuance and, without even acknowledging my IP; one speaker even commented on my "remarkable understanding of the model" before being informed by others why that might be! This highlights the dangers of insufficient understanding and accidental suboptimization. Let's analyze what we can predict is likely to happen when parts of an integrated system such as RME are implemented.

Predicted Consequences of Partial Implementation

Whyte's (2001) dissertation highlights the dangers of selective implementation (Table 10.1). He noted the danger of relying solely on the leadership aspects of change without the necessary leverage provided by both a Continuous Improvement program and employee engagement. How can we mitigate these outcomes? A useful antidote is the organizational development (OD) "rejected premise principle."

The Rejected Premise Principle

Life is not like in the movies, so a fully leveraged option is not always possible. An invaluable OD principle states, "Once a decision

TABLE 10.1 **Impact of Partial Implementation**

Mass Engagement and Enablement	Cathedral/ Higher Purpose Model of Leadership	"Predict and Prevent" Continuous Improvement of the Right Things	Predicted Consequences
✓	✓	✓	Leveraged systematic excellence.
✓	✗	✓	Leadership skills' variation undermines the new bottom-up culture, but CI systems discipline gradually erodes the variation. Big opportunity cost re pace. Scientific mindset is reliant totally on CI systems *rather than being systematically supported by leadership.*
✓	✗	✗	The new culture is quickly undermined by variation in leadership and lack of depth of scientific mindset leading to disillusionment.
✓	✓	✗	The emotional ownership and leadership quality sustains the culture but is frustrated by lack of CI systems so the effort suboptimizes and frustrates highly motivated staff.
✗	✓	✓	CI and leadership gradually create and sustain a new culture, but it is slower (opportunity cost) and is always seen as the organization's system rather than being deeply and widely owned by employees.
✗	✗	✓	A CI culture can evolve but it is constantly undermined by the variation in leadership and depends solely on process for sustainability.
✗	✓	✗	The quality and alignment of the leadership gradually creates and sustains a new culture, but it is slower (opportunity cost) and lacks the depth of emotional ownership achieved by mass engagement. It is thus less robust in response to senior management changes, etc. Scientific mindset is reliant solely on leadership quality rather than being systematically supported by CI systems and culture.

has been made to choose an option, the weaknesses in the chosen option will be found in the strengths of the rejected options."

Applying this principle, if your organization cannot implement the full leverage possible from the three focus areas (engagement, leadership, and Continuous Improvement), examine the missing part of the formula and strengthen it in some other way. This can be done by mitigation or substitution, but the aim is to satisfactorily reduce the predicted suboptimization caused by partial implementation. If you can't implement X, analyze what X provides and find an alternative way if providing it.

One bulwark against suboptimization is a strict discipline in implementing and sustaining high standards. This cannot happen if individuals cannot remember what those standards are and how to deliver them, so let's explore how to make content memorable in the next chapter.

CHAPTER 11

Opening the Door for Logic and Science

Learning can only happen when a child is interested. If he's not interested, it's like throwing marshmallows at his head and calling it eating.

Unknown
Attributed to Katrina Gutleben

Human beings love to laugh; let's examine why this is crucial to the success of RME.

Serious Issues and Fun

At the end of a night shift RME workshop in 2015, my co-facilitator and I were shaking hands with participants as they left. A small group approached, arm-in-arm and smiling broadly; one proclaimed: "This is the best night out we've had for years!" Many years earlier, writer G. K. Chesterton is said to have noted, "Humor can get in under the door while seriousness is still fumbling at the handle."

So why run workshops in a manner designed to be fun as well as serious? My short answer is that life is too short not to! Let's begin the longer answer by exploring the impact of two conflicting leadership messages.

Two Conflicting Messages

Senior leaders regularly communicate *both* of the messages shown in Figure 11.1 to employees.

FIGURE 11.1 **Conflicting Messages**

Message #1
"Speak up"

Employees are told to speak up, to expose any wrongdoings, to use whistleblower avenues, to ensure bad stuff is exposed, and to engage in fear-free discussions about issues.

Message #2
"Don't speak up"

Employees are also told not to say anything if there is a theoretical possibility that someone somewhere might be offended by what they say.

Given these opposite messages, why are we surprised that employees hesitate to speak up? When employees report lack of trust in their senior leadership, these conflicting messages are often referenced. Both messages are well meaning, but the employee feedback is damning. A typical recent example was a manager, early in a workshop, who said, "Don't ask me to be honest and open when, if I use the 'wrong' word, I am going to be accused of racism or some other 'ism' and have my career ruined." By the end of that workshop, however, he and his colleagues were freely contributing and had a more nuanced appreciation of the good intentions of both senior leaders and HR colleagues. The open discussion also gave them hope as they experienced the exploration of ideas without chilling debate and sacrificing honesty.

In a 2022 workshop a manager said, "This is the first time since I joined this organization that I have felt able to genuinely express my evaluation of the issues holding us back. Thank you." He felt this way despite his organization's whistleblower charter and mechanisms. This is dispiriting for all those working to protect whistleblowers and create cultures that value the unhindered exploration of ideas and concepts so crucial to high rates of innovation and improvement. How do we combat this erosion of healthy debate?

The wide and deep facilitation capability outlined in Chapter 9 is crucial here; having highly skilled internal facilitators working in every area and shift enables difficult conversations to happen skillfully. These peer group conversations are less inhibited than those with managers and result in less guarded and therefore more accurate expressions of what employees really think and feel. In a wider societal context, it explicitly provides a healthy and informal alternative to the tendency to find more and more subject matters problematic.

Think of the following vision for your own organization. Imagine the effect of widespread, mutually respectful, and skilled conversations. Your employees are not afraid of exploring new ideas and concepts. Imagine the reduction in divisiveness if your culture modeled the common RME Behavioral Standard of "Assume positive intent."* Imagine the impact that atmosphere would have on the enjoyability of coming to work, the attraction and retention of cognitively diverse employees, and on innovation. Let's see what happens if we fail to create an environment where people's ideas and creativity can be freely expressed.

---

* What the French call *bienveillance*.

How Overcaution Damages Learning Capability and Competitiveness

The "don't speak up" message has several unintended consequences, and one of the most damaging is the effect on training and learning material, as shown in Figure 11.2.

FIGURE 11.2 **How Overcaution Damages Learning and Competitiveness**

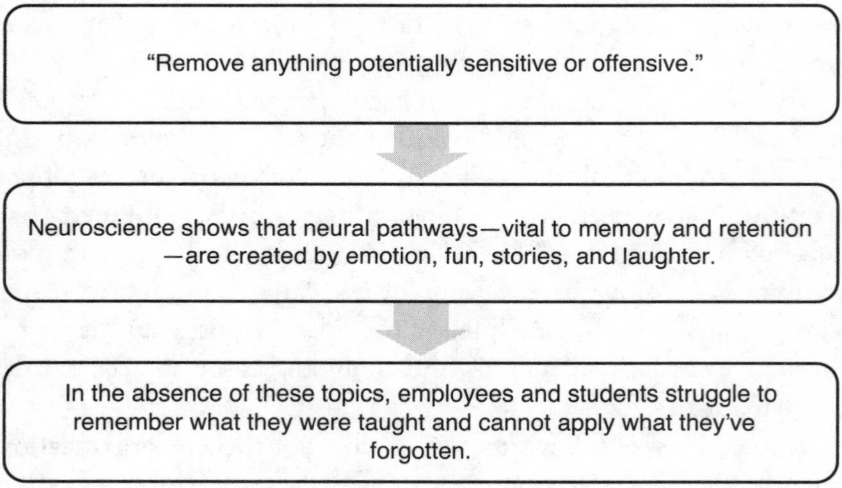

"Remove anything potentially sensitive or offensive."

Neuroscience shows that neural pathways—vital to memory and retention—are created by emotion, fun, stories, and laughter.

In the absence of these topics, employees and students struggle to remember what they were taught and cannot apply what they've forgotten.

The key challenge to those who design educational and business learning is that if material is overcautious it becomes boring and hard to remember. When this happens, it prompts the brain to respond like a willful teenager and say, "This is boring, why should I create any neural pathways for this, why would I ever want to remember such drivel?"

Similarly, how can we create world-class competitive organizations if we accidently design our training material to be difficult to remember? While this is only one factor in a complex set of issues, if we adopt an overcautious zeal to strip out most of the elements that our brains find interesting, those of us in the West should not be surprised when we discover disappointing outcomes in international educational comparisons compared to societies not afflicted with this intellectual timidity.*

In summary, ensure that the "speak out" message is your dominant narrative, embrace the role of fun in learning, and proudly and assertively reverse the prevailing stultifying caution about the types of conversations adults are capable of having. Let's build on that foundation by exploring the roles of curiosity, vivid language, and stories in opening minds to logic and science.

Curiosity

One of the many ways the entertainment industry grabs our attention is to create curiosity. At the end of Season 1 of *Game of Thrones*, a big-name star has his head cut off despite a deal to save his life. Viewers think, "Wow, I didn't expect that to happen" and pay attention. The producers are smart—they want us to watch Season 2.

RME is designed to create curiosity by stimulating employees to ask themselves questions such as "Will management really do this?" and "Will they give us the power to make these decisions?" Earlier, we explored how important it was to quickly undermine cynicism and the peer-group status of cynics. This undermining happens as outcomes are achieved that cynics have loudly proclaimed as "impossible." This in turn invites wonder about what will happen next.

Overall, RME stimulates the "this is interesting" response, like the reaction to an unexpected plot development in a play or movie or good story line of any type. Curiosity gets attention and creates anticipation for what is coming next, namely the scientific and

---

* Such as the OECD's PISA or the Program for International Student Assessment.

logical aspects of RME, which otherwise may not "land" for many employees. Consider how much time organizations spend preparing communication to send to employees compared to the time preparing employees to be receptive. Organizational communication is often like a farmer who invests heavily in the best seeds and then hires a helicopter to scatter these expensive seeds onto unprepared land! I think we can predict the success of that crop.

Similarly, if employees are not listening it doesn't matter how well-crafted messages are; they haven't got employees' attention. We must spend the time to open the door for our messages to reach employees. Curiosity helps create that initial opening. So does vivid language.

Vivid Language

A Johnson & Johnson senior leader described the liberating effect of his first management RME workshop in this way:

> In corporate settings people worry about saying the wrong thing, and feedback, and openness to feedback, suffers. You completely removed that by your continued soliciting of, and openness to, feedback and by your use of vivid language. We felt the rules had changed for the better, we became unburdened and comfortable to say what we needed to say. Our filters were removed and that exposed the emotion that people have inside.

Earlier we saw how making learning material overcautious also makes it harder for our brains to access it when needed. In *King Lear*, Shakespeare knew the visual and auditory effect of Gloucester's eyes being gouged out would shock audiences and be memorable. But he added vivid language to the mix. Cornwall shouts, "Out, vile jelly!" as he gouges out Gloucester's second eye and smears his cheeks with the remnants.

During the 2008–2010 recession, one factory had an issue when native UK employees were made redundant but higher-skilled Polish employees kept their jobs. This caused resentment that escalated into vandalism of Polish employees' cars and other hostility toward them.

To counter this underground activity, I trained the leaders in the factory to use vivid language. They addressed the issue with the workforce by stressing how important highly skilled technicians and engineers were to the competitiveness of the factory and to preserving as many jobs as possible. We crafted some key questions to ask during formal and informal interactions, especially with those suspected of creating hostility. A specific, deliberately provocative, vivid language question asked was, "Would you rather have Polish workers doing British jobs in the United Kingdom or Polish workers doing British jobs in Poland?" Once this question was asked in numerous group conversations, people understood, and all hostile incidents ceased.

In another case, a previously independent business was acquired by a global corporation. As corporate policies and systems were implemented, the local senior team complained about perceived corporate interference and bureaucracy. They expressed open resentment toward their new corporate bosses. They all, however, vividly remembered what it was like to be ruled by the Soviet Union. To address this issue the CEO, trained in vivid language, replied to anti-corporate comments by saying: "We must visit the Soviet Union before the Soviet Union visits us." Her senior team understood the analogy and the new power dynamics; stakeholder engagement improved dramatically.

In both examples, large organizational benefits were achieved quickly by stimulating reflection via vivid language. For RME, this is taught as part of the facilitator training for both Behavioral Standards and leadership facilitators. It is also used for senior teams needing to overcome communication challenges such as those outlined above. Let's build further on the power of emotion.

First Emotion, Only Then Logic and Science

In the early days of cell phones, the expansion of the US market lagged compared to some other markets. In response, a cell phone provider ran an advertisement in which, on two successive mornings, a young child ran to his mother as she left for work. He wanted to show her something he had done. Both times she gently explained that she had to go "to see the client." When this repeated on the third day, the child asked, "When can I be the client?" The advertisement then switched scenes to the mother chatting from work with her son on her new cell phone.

The technique here is communications laddering, reaching people at an emotional level first, and only then, when you have piqued their interest, introducing the logical benefits of the proposal or idea. In RME, creating an authentic Higher Purpose begins to move people emotionally, as they think about their families and communities. Once RME gains momentum, the genuine acts of kindness and courage that follow add to this effect. Stories addressing key issues such as the need for consensus, not compromise, and the dangers of cynicism add to this momentum, creating an opening for logic.

Stories

I have emphasized the importance of measuring the impact of interventions against tangible outcomes that move the dial. In their *Harvard Business Review* article, Nielsen and McCullough (2018) neatly blend this with storytelling:

> The data analysis found that teams whose managers spent at least 16 minutes of one-to-one time with each direct per week had 30% more engaged direct reports than the average manager who spent just 9 minutes per week with directs. When they brought that data-driven story to the front lines,

suddenly a platitude was transformed into a useful bench-mark that got the attention of managers.

Only a minority of stories are data centric. The stories employees repeat back to me are often deeply emotional and/or relate to family, values, and the history of local communities. Like the European Heineken advert with the catchphrase "We reach the parts other beers cannot reach," these stories reached those parts also, the parts that drive discretionary effort and a high-performance culture.

Earlier we saw how the working mother's story drove cell phone sales. Andy Brammer, now a general manager in Kerry Foods, remarked that he has always remembered the train story told as part of the Bacardi RME, the impact it had on his subsequently award-winning site, and on him as a young first line leader.

The train story is introduced in the initial RME employee work-shops if individuals are being uncharitable toward other individuals or departments. The story is that a man boards a quiet train carriage with four young children under 10 years old. They occupy a table section, and the kids begin to amuse themselves. This creates noise. The father meanwhile sits motionless. As his children's play becomes louder, he does nothing.

The noise continues and other travelers stare at him and make easily overheard comments like "You would think the father would have some consideration for others." This pattern continues until one man approaches the father who is sitting with his head in his hands. The aggrieved passenger tells the father, "Your children are disrupting others. You need to take charge."

The father looks up, apologizes, and immediately quiets his children. He looks up again at the man and says, "We were at the hospital. Their mother has just died. I was thinking of her."

Assuming positive intent in situations like this is difficult, but leader after leader interviewed for this book attest to the power-ful impact of introducing stories to their locations. The stories are like guided missiles targeted against cynicism, negative and limit-ing assumptions, catastrophizing, and so on. They form part of the internal facilitator training and equip local facilitators to create new stories that resonate with the local history and culture. They also relate to topical events, in sport, in drama, in foreign affairs or politics thus ensuring both memorability and the face validity key for credibility.

In summary, stories reach people at emotional levels unattainable by science and logic; key is to leverage emotion to enable the science and logic to be effective. I have included some other stories below which, if you like them, you can adapt to your own organization, and if you don't, no harm has been done!

Example Stories

The stories that follow were remembered fondly by people interviewed for this book. As you read them, notice what made them memorable even many years later. Given natural human and cultural variability, tastes will differ, but if everyone is pleased to see others smile, we will all have a better working environment with fewer judgments, more understanding, and more charity.

Two Sisters, One Orange, and the Limits of Compromise

When employees are introduced to the need for consensus, there is often skepticism around why we can't just speed things up with compromise or majority voting; some even suspect that I am paid by the hour and am introducing unnecessary extra work!

When this happens, I stress that to reach consensus we need to ensure we understand why someone is adopting a particular position so we can generate ways of addressing what really matters to the other person. That is the logical explanation, and if it is insufficient to convince the group I tell the story of the two sisters and the orange.

It is a Sunday evening, and all the shops are closed. Two sisters argue about who should have the last orange. Eventually they decide to compromise and reach for a knife and cut the orange in half. One sister stays in the kitchen, and other goes to her room. The latter peels her half orange and discards the peel. The sister who remained in the kitchen removes and discards the orange from the peel she needs to bake her cake, which now has to be a smaller cake. If only they had used consensus.

"My People Are My Most Important Asset" Really?

Coca-Cola's Steve Thorpe was sent to run a low-performing site. When taking over a site, Steve's leader standard work includes quickly diagnosing the level of commitment among his new team to employee engagement and to raise it decisively and quickly if required.

In his first discussion with one of his shift managers, he was told "my people are my most important asset." As the conversation continued, Steve asked him for the asset care plan for a particular piece of packaging equipment. The shift manager proudly produced a detailed asset care plan with up-to-date data and demonstrated in-depth technical knowledge of every aspect of it. He explained that he had asset care plans and data for every piece of equipment in the factory. Steve smiled and said, "OK, let's move from equipment to people and go through individual employees and discuss your detailed plans and recent conversations with each."

Steve asked about a series of named individuals and found much less detail. There was a remarkably similar and generic response about everyone. The shift manager learned quickly and with no resistance to the increase in conversational workload required. This demonstrated that the issue was simply one of reframing the role of a leader. The shift manager learned the value of conversational "Quality × Quantity" as depicted in the CHPM.

Diana Ross and the HRs

HR professionals, unfairly in many cases, are not regarded as the best companions for a good night out. When I worked with Bacardi it had two senior HR professionals, Colleen Potter and Helen Early, who jointly led the department following the removal of their previous boss. He had proved unsuitable to lead the new cultural and leadership standards introduced following Consensus Day. They both championed the intellectual challenge and freedom introduced by the RME reforms of HR policy and practice. This included embracing the philosophy of taking our work, but not ourselves, seriously.

As an example, they sometimes broke into spontaneous singing when a word or concept in a discussion reminded either of a song they liked. One day, the happy news of someone's pregnancy led to an immediate and joyous rendition of "Baby Love" by Diana Ross & The Supremes!

That HR department was one of the most well respected and effective I have ever had the pleasure to work with. Employees were relaxed about approaching HR with issues ,and the site was placed in the top 10 in the UK's Best Companies to Work For employee engagement assessment for five successive years.*

In Chapter 12 we will see Herb Kelleher describe the kind of "professionals" that drove Southwest Airlines' results. You will see that Herb would have loved Helen and Colleen.

"Please Don't Do That!"

Halma's Rob Lewis, now a regional managing director, rang me in 2018. He was assembling his global team in Barcelona and asked how much of the CHPM skills I could teach them in the two days he had made available in the agenda. We agreed on the best use of the time available, and I casually mentioned that I was aware that the world was a more sensitive place than when we last worked together and that I had adjusted my style to accommodate this increase in sensitivity. Rob shouted, amiably, into the phone, "No, no please don't do that; I want them to get exactly what I got years ago. I want them to remember it all, just like I do!"

We reached an amiable compromise, and we laugh about it to this day!

---

* https://awards-list.co.uk/sunday_times_100_best_companies_great_place.

"It Worked for Jack Nicholson"

In the movie *As Good as It Gets*, the socially inept Jack Nicholson ruins his first date and Helen Hunt begins to walk out; he implores her to stay, and she shouts: "Pay me a compliment!" He does, and the rest is history.

In Chapter 7, we saw that one of the arrows in the CHPM signified the need to earn the right before moving to the right in the model. Boston Scientific's Enda Colleran tells this story.

> As a team, we frequently reminded ourselves about earning the right, but one day, one of my peers was giving a colleague feedback that was in public and not very constructive. The recipient of this tirade smiled at his accuser and said:
>
> "Pay me a compliment!"
>
> It worked just as well for him as for Helen Hunt . . . we all fell about laughing, we resolved the issue, and the incident bonded us together and it reminded us about how feedback should be given!

How Unintended Consequences Countered Smugness

Early in my career, my wages manager, accustomed to paying employees on Fridays, came to me and said, "The bank can't get the money into people's accounts until tomorrow." Tomorrow was Saturday, and I knew that many employees paid bills on Friday night. It was Friday afternoon, so the decision was taken to get cash from the bank and make up old-style pay packets for every one of the 1,000+ employees while canceling the electronic transfers. We gathered all our managers together and divided the workforce between us. We delivered wages to everyone by 7 p.m.

When the final manager rang me to confirm delivery, I relaxed for the weekend, smugly satisfied that I had done a good job. On Monday I had a string of complaints from employees. Apparently not everyone is transparent about their earnings, and the complainants had experienced some uncomfortable conversations when their partners learned how much they were earning. You just can't win sometimes.

Irony and Setting Expectations

The CHPM leadership program that supports RME includes a phase called Setting Expectations and Managing Overcommitment (see Chapter 7). This covers how to be very behaviorally specific and clear when setting expectations. It is a pity my grandad had not been trained this way when he established his business in the 1920s.

Earlier I mentioned my grandparents escaped Belfast under threat in the Irish Revolutionary and Civil War period. In addition to having to abandon his house, my grandfather also lost his job at Harland & Wolff following the expulsion of Catholics, and those married to Catholics, from the shipyards in 1920. He set up a construction business just across the new Irish border in Belturbet, County Cavan.

In the 1920s construction work was overwhelmingly on a "no work–no pay" basis. Grandad created a small team of highly skilled tradesmen who traveled with him from job to job across Ireland and Great Britain. Their loyalty was deepened by grandad being one of the first employers to pay "wet money" to maintain some employee income when they could not work due to adverse weather. On every local site he augmented his core team with additional local tradesmen and unskilled laborers. He used a one-week probationary period to assess the latter's suitability.

One laborer was late on day one and became progressively more late each morning until he rolled into work on Friday 20 minutes late. My grandad was waiting for him. The conversation went like this:

> GRANDAD (WITH IRONY IN HIS VOICE): "So you can come to work anytime you like?"
>
> DOFFING HIS CAP, THE MAN REPLIED: "Thank you very much Mr. Devine, they said you were a real gentleman, thank you very much I really appreciate that" as he strode, unhurriedly into work. As my mother recalled, "Daddy didn't have the heart to fire him."

The story had a happy ending. When the building was complete the Town Council held a civic reception for grandad and his team.

Grandad was sitting with the local dignitaries over dinner when he got a message that there was someone at the door who wanted to see him. When he went downstairs, he saw the local laborer standing there with a bottle of Jameson whiskey for him.* The man said: "Thank you for giving me a chance Mr. Devine, no one had ever done that before." He then grinned and, as he walked away, he winked at grandad saying, "And I now know how important it is to get to work on time!"

Let's now leave the land of stories and conclude with an Executive Summary in the form of the Key Success Factors for RME in the next chapter.

---

* An expensive gift for a working man in the 1920s.

RME Key Success Factors

*If you are thinking of rolling this out, we
have failed to explain it to you.*

Employee advice to an executive visitor to an RME site

This chapter summarizes the main key success factors for implementing RME and any similar attempt to rapidly increase employee engagement and enablement.

Decide If RME Is Appropriate

RME begins with the senior team Diagnostic Day. It is surprising how often leaders are willing to abandon collective responsibility when major changes encounter inevitable challenges and difficulties. For this reason, it is critical that every member of the senior team attends the Diagnostic Day and that the decisions are made by consensus, not compromise or majority voting. This ensures that when the inevitable pressure to deviate from the Joint Change Plan agreed on with the workforce happens, it is very difficult for any weak-kneed individual to bleat, "I didn't agree to it."

What does this diagnostic and decision-making day achieve? The team reaches consensus on what the organization is trying to achieve, the detailed scope, what degree of employee engagement and enablement is required to achieve this, the current levels of employee engagement, and the current leadership and Continuous Improvement capability.

The senior team also considers what options are available using benchmarked examples and agrees the best option in the circumstances. The workshop also decides how to frame the intervention in ways that maximize initial employee face validity. Teams also decides how to signal the integrity and commitment necessary to achieve success.

I encourage discussion of the likelihood of policy innovation as the inputs of the entire workforce create new options. This is particularly significant for policies that impact employees' experience of their daily work such as HR, communication, and quality. If the professional gatekeepers are open to innovation and challenge, these policies benefit from the cold reality of direct employee experience constructively disrupting often well-meaning but end user–unfriendly current policies and procedures. A team that embraces end-user engagement will discover it drives innovation through the organization and even back to original equipment suppliers in the supply chain. This extends the benefits beyond the organization's borders and strengthens the market for consumers of these products and services. Some leaders see these sector-changing opportunities immediately; some take longer; some never see the full potential of RME. I recommend you join the first group.

During the Diagnostic Day, consensus is not guaranteed, and the most senior leader must be satisfied—in follow-up one-on-one discussion with individual colleagues—that there is complete ownership of the process by all members of the senior team. Superficial unanimity is not enough to withstand the inevitable turmoil as engaged employees and improvement momentum clash with vested interests and lack of imagination. When genuine commitment is absent, I have advised potential clients not to proceed; I do so because raising employee expectations and then failing to meet them increases cynicism and makes future attempts harder to succeed. Sometimes the frank discussion of the commitment deficit results in individuals leaving the senior team.

In one case we had to change the design to minimize the exposure of one senior leader to the workforce pending moves to find him a job elsewhere. In others, I have withdrawn from the process at this stage, explaining that without genuine commitment it is better to slow down or even stop, rather than to proceed quickly with a team likely to fragment under the inevitable pressure of implementation. This feedback is not always well received, especially by leaders whose style is to "go quickly to go quickly."

Sometimes the senior team issue is not lack of commitment but genuine disagreement. RME is unnecessarily risky when a senior team is not sufficiently aligned about how much employee engagement is needed to achieve ambitious organizational goals. Better to build that alignment first, then regroup and go again. This has worked well in some of the RME examples covered earlier where the senior leader has had the humility to "go slow to go quick" and come back to me with variations of "Remember you told me to work on my team? Well I did, and now we are ready to start."

An excellent example of building that consensus was Boston Scientific's decision in 2015 to broaden consensus beyond the senior team to include a much broader group of leaders. This was done not only to widen ownership of the decision that RME was appropriate but also to create the site's Higher Purpose.

Finally, the market situation of an organization may make it unsuitable for RME. I advise against RME when the organization is not seeking significant improvement in performance. The step change in improvement can be to move even further ahead of competitors, overtake strong competitors, or overcome an immediate threat or crisis; in all situations hunger to improve must run through the veins of the senior team. RME is not for the complacent. I also advise against RME when significant changes in the senior team are anticipated within two years (see Chapter 10). If you reach consensus that RME is appropriate, a key issue is how to maximize integrity and trust.

Demonstrate Integrity and Build Trust

Integrity has to be demonstrated, and trust has to be earned. Two practical steps to achieving this follow.

If You Wish the Ends, You Must Mandate the Means

Leaders often learn from trusted others that RME is working well in a particular location and arrange to visit to see for themselves. They encounter proud employees who show them how their Behavioral Standards make work enjoyable and productive, the changes they have made, and so on. Some of these visitors then contact me enthused about the level of discretionary effort and passion they have experienced. They are keen to achieve similar outcomes for their organization.

If they are seriously considering RME, I recommend the senior team Diagnostic Day discussed previously. On that day the contrast with conventional approaches to culture change is thoroughly discussed. Key is to ensure the strength of ambitious goals is matched by the strength of the mechanism chosen to deliver them. During the Diagnostic Day, many leaders discover that this strength alignment has been absent in previous attempts at achieving significant culture change. Employees are often presented with ambitious statements of cultural intent, but when they sit through the PowerPoint blitz, they frequently discover it is risk-averse and emotionally underwhelming. In contrast, the goals these cultural initiatives are supposed to deliver are transformational. This contrast, the timidity of the means to achieve ambitious ends, is the opposite of what is needed to build trust.

Given this, why do people express surprise that so many employees are skeptical and even cynical? Skepticism in such circumstances is a sign of intelligence. To employees, their bosses have decided they wish the ends but are not prepared to mandate the means.

In summary, the ambition of the objectives must be matched by the power of the engagement process necessary to achieve it. It is to the great credit of all the organizations and individuals mentioned in this book that when presented with culture change/engagement options they chose the most challenging ones, the ones that required total integrity and a willingness to work far outside their comfort zones.

Earn Employee Trust

At conferences, senior leaders sometimes say to me:

> Allowing the employees to determine the agenda for Consensus Day and to design the new culture sounds risky. Isn't there a way you can manipulate it to ensure we get what we want?

Doing the exact opposite is what builds trust in the process. In Chapter 1 we saw how the type of mutually respectful, nonhierarchical, and psychologically safe conversations maximized during RME gradually and cumulatively build employee trust in the process.

When considering RME, trust is built by employees talking to their peers in locations where RME has already been implemented. At the start of RME, fear is reduced and trust is built by separating employees from managers in the initial diagnostic phases, when fear of reprisal is strong. As trust grows, RME safely reunites employees and their management at Consensus Day and thereafter.

Fundamental RME design features become important here as employees notice unexpected details such as that the senior team workshop is the only RME workshop that does not have the power to put any items on the Consensus Day agenda. In the days before

Consensus Day, the way in which employees elected by their employee workshops are prepared for Consensus Day by the facilitator, and the complete transparency of the data collected from all workshops, add to this trust momentum. At Consensus Day, people see the use of verbatim wording and quotes with explicitly no censorship of employees' chosen words. Trust is further built by the visually clear employee majority and how Consensus Day is facilitated.

As Consensus Day wrestles with the prioritized issues, trust increases. The collective diagnosis and problem-solving during Consensus Day and afterward deepen organizational and commercial understanding; in so doing empathy for those in other departments and doing other jobs increases; this impacts attitudes to managers. The stories circulating in the workforce that all Consensus Day decisions were taken in the open, with the explicit and enforced banning of the type of adjournments and side meetings common in negotiations, send the message that it is very different. In turn this encourages curiosity and open-mindedness.

Employee trust also grows when workers see their individual behavioral data explicitly reflected in the new Behavioral Standards. When a team of employee facilitators from all job roles begin training employees in the new Behavioral Standards, this reinforces the "this is for real" message and further builds trust; this minimization of hierarchy, also experienced in the tightly aligned leadership and Continuous Improvement approaches, adds to this impact.

Cumulatively, trust is built by each of the above RME design features. These can be implemented separately by your organization but are much more effective if they leverage each other in a rapid series of events.

In the early stages of RME, I am frequently on-site training leaders, and I chat with many employees as I purposefully walk around; I have frequently been told that the cumulative effect of all of the above gave employees evidence to base their trust on; they are keen to tell me this is the opposite of blind faith in management!

Maximize Corporate Support

RME is tough. Things go wrong when attempting to do things never done before. When there is a setback, it is important that corporate leaders understand and support the effort. This can be achieved in several ways.

Rolls-Royce included members of the Civil Aerospace senior team in their separate local Consensus Days. This provided experiential and emotional support for local leaders and facilitators. Other organizations have included key corporate leaders in the process of evaluation prior to the senior team Diagnostic Day. Worries that corporate values will be compromised by Behavioral Standards are addressed in this way. These fears have always proved to be unfounded but are real until proven otherwise.

Avoid Unnecessary Standardization and Let a Thousand Flowers Bloom

Standardization is crucial to establish and improve standards, but there must be a performance rationale independent of neatness and uniformity, and one that is more powerful than the loss of ownership and innovation inevitable with standardization. This trade-off is infrequently considered by central functions.

We saw in Chapter 6 how lazy standardization destroys engagement. For corporate leaders, the ability to compare the performance of different organizational units is crucial for effective capital investment allocation, for executive succession planning, and for regulatory compliance.

Neatness and uniformity both facilitate comparison. Standardization for its own sake thus becomes popular. In turn, this leads to attempts to "roll out" initiatives in a uniform, "we know best" manner. We saw in Chapter 6 that it is important to operate with the optimal mix of integration and differentiation. Bias toward standardization is a bias toward integration over differentiation and is thus a source of predictable suboptimization.

As a corporate leader, I designed draft training materials for self-directed work teams. The challenge was how to optimize the engagement of local teams across the globe by adapting to wide variations in local cultural dimensions (see Hofstede 2010) and histories. We found that "HQ knows best" had led to shallow acquiescence, which had predictable consequences for performance and engagement. The lesson was that we needed to escape our Western, specifically Northern European, cultural bubble.* A better approach is to respect local culture by giving a different kind of direction such as:

> Here is what our (corporate) research tells us and how it has worked in these cultures. Please take this learning, adapt it to your local culture and experiment, keep us informed about what is working and what isn't and about any diagnoses of root causes. Our aim is to let a thousand flowers bloom locally so that all of us can learn more and improve via exchange of best practice.

This is an example of "wanted variability," the variability that it is not useful to try to eliminate by standardization (Kahneman, Sibony, and Sunstein 2021). It is wanted because it maximizes ownership, engagement, enablement, and innovation with no loss of quality.

When senior visitors are being shown around RME locations, employees patiently explain why rollout or "cut and paste" approaches miss the point. Their attempts to avoid superficial copying often conflict with the confirmation bias built up by many years of habitual top-down and rollout thinking. Remember the polite employee notice from Chapter 6? "Warning: attempts to apply

---

* If you are reading this in Asia or Africa, please test these recommendations against your experiences of working for Western-owned organizations and join this discussion.

these standards without the process that created them will only disappoint!"

How can you roll out something that is built on unique local organizational and individual experiences and history? How can you roll out an organizational culture that uses the specific local language of the specific, differentiated location? How can the depth of ownership created by RME be replicated top-down? RME depends for its authenticity on the emergent decisions made by an entire workforce on an agenda created by that workforce, not by a workforce somewhere else. As the issues will be different location by location, it is impossible to achieve the same results by a standardized top-down approach.

To summarize, let's listen to the advice one employee gave to a very senior visitor: "If you are thinking of rolling this out, we have failed to explain it to you."

Take the Time Necessary to Understand RME, Especially Its Emergent Nature

RME is emergent. It is difficult to fully understand in advance. Time spent making the RME facilitator available to key leadership groups and union representatives (where appropriate) helps establish the face validity and integrity of the process prior to the initial employee workshops. As an excellent example of best practice, Boston Scientific spent many months arranging mini workshops to enable key stakeholders to test RME's credibility and deeply understand the process prior to committing to it.

Understand the Limits of Engagement

A key reason employee diagnostic workshops produce such accurate results is that we are asking employees to engage on issues they are expert on.* Employees know what stops them from doing a good job, what repeat failures happen, and what kind of leadership fails to inspire them.

Diagnostic accuracy is necessary but not sufficient for effective problem solving. The best solutions to dealing with the diagnosed issues are usually outside the prior experience of managers and employees alike; they cannot be accessed by experience alone. Therefore, Consensus Day, and the subsequent detailed projects arising from it, need skillful problem-solving and other Continuous Improvement capability. Engagement alone is not sufficient.

Define Process and Scope Tightly

Sometimes senior people walk around a site where RME has been implemented and return to their organizations and attempt to achieve the same results without conducting the rigorous analysis and consensus-building that takes place on the senior team Diagnostic Day. This includes a meticulous definition of scope.

Poorly defined scope fails to set realistic employee expectations or priorities and is guaranteed to disappoint. Furthermore, senior management, faced with unserious but emotive suggestions, row back and feebly argue "but we can't do that because . . ." It is far better to have adult-adult and commercially literate discussions with employees from the start. The initial RME employee workshops set this adult-adult expectation and clearly communicate scope.

A lesson can be learned from Western trips to Japan in the early 1980s when industrial tourists came back and implemented Quality Circles. This superficial implementation was within the structural and cultural norms of their existing operating systems. Many had

---

* It was the consistent nature of this feedback from thousands of employees on many different sites that led me to question the way we train our leaders. See Chapter 7.

failed to understand the philosophy and culture that made Quality Circles successful in Japan.*

Manage Expectations but Maximize Solution Space

As we saw previously, conventional approaches to changing culture tend to be risk-averse. As an example of this mentality, I am involved, as a sponsor and volunteer, in a "broken window theory" (Wilson and Kelling 1982) type urban renewal initiative in a deprived city. I recently overheard a communications manager respond to a simple request to publicly thank a crew of street cleaners for working with residents to clean up communal spaces. He responded by asking, "Are we sure naming them will not cause offense? Don't we need them to sign a written consent form allowing us to name them publicly?"

I had to control myself from interjecting, "How many working people do you know who get offended by being appreciated for their work?" After being recognized, far from being offended, the crew increased its initiative and discretionary effort. The crew members even insisted on continuing to clean up communal spaces when invited to celebrate with residents after work!

Risk-aversion is common when senior teams realize how much power is transferred to employees in RME. This is a danger point because if the scope is too risk-averse, solution space can become too small to engage employees deeply enough. If solution space is unnecessarily restricted, the significance of the decisions employees are trusted to make is correspondingly reduced. This has predictable consequences on engagement.

You might argue that I have warned that the limits to engagement need to be understood; this is true, but key here is that within

* Peter Wickens's account of how Nissan's UK senior team immersed itself in lean philosophy and practice before they opened their new factory is revealing here—see Wickens 1987.

those limits, the more solution space the more engagement. How are these superficially conflicting imperatives resolved?

In the senior team diagnostic workshop, once the diagnosis is complete, we move to designing the intervention necessary to deliver the objectives clarified. The "sweet spot" here is ensuring the scope is clear so that expectations are managed, while maximizing solution space. It is crucial that the senior team does not commit to implementing decisions outside its own authority. Sharing power with employees does create engagement, but the senior team can only share the power that it has. For example, local senior teams rarely have 100 percent control of pay and benefits policy and decisions. Once scope is clear and detailed, we work to maximize solution space by challenging every proposed limitation and only reducing solution space for very clear, defined, and defensible reasons.

This discussion itself helps diagnose the extent of hunger for change and alignment within the senior team. That diagnosis sometimes leads to the decision from me, or the organization, not to initiate RME but to design a less radical option or to cease the activity.

Choosing a less radical option has predictable consequences for the level of engagement achieved subsequently and on the pace of culture change. Analytically this may be appropriate in the circumstances, but it can cause a feeling of emotional loss within senior teams who, by this stage, understand the potential of RME but also realize they are not yet ready to achieve it.

I have walked away from large commercial opportunities on that basis. Integrity is crucial.

Understand the Power of Consensus Day

How does it feel walking into Consensus Day as a senior leader? You see a mass of employees elected by their workshops, gathered for the first time; they outnumber your team by at least two to one. They look at you and wonder how you are going to react. Will you engage with their feedback and their arguments? You know that what you say and don't say will be intensely scrutinized for evidence of intent and commitment. You wonder about your own team: are any only superficially committed, will any desert under fire in the months to come? What happens if this fails? Chris Thomson, then general manager of Vale's Clydach Refinery, reflected:

> The start of Consensus Day was a strange experience because, as a member of senior management, I was uncertain what my role would be, but I knew that I would be "on show" in front of the entire workforce. Normally this wouldn't be an issue, but we were all unsure about where the conversations would go, and what challenging situations we would be forced to confront. The fact that we were in an unusual environment with 50+ people from all departments and organizational levels set exactly the right tone; it made it a level playing field for all participants. This was important, both symbolically and in creating a safe environment for all to speak. A strong facilitator was absolutely essential to ensure everyone had their say but also that people didn't hog the floor and to ensure that everyone was accountable for what they said. There are people in both managerial and workforce positions that like to make sweeping, throw-away comments, but here, every comment had to be justified. This was important because, without it, it would have been far easier to influence those attendees who would take words on face value if it substantiated their previously held opinions. Myths were exposed in a manner that was respectful to the opinions held. The approach of 100 percent consensus being agreed, with a conscious hand vote every time, was crucial; it was impossible to be a bystander during Consensus Day, which was critical for providing the requisite credibility to the final Joint Change Plan.

Consensus Day is more than just agreement by consensus— it delivers widespread curiosity and thus openness, it quickly undermines cynicism, and it accelerates momentum. It also human-izes senior management in the eyes of employees. Cross-functionally, representatives deeply empathize with their colleagues in other functions as they listen to their frustrations and work with them to diagnose and then problem solve to create the Joint Change Plan.

The effect on the organization is that representatives, by own-ing the decisions made, become a collective change agent. This significantly broadens the coalition for change and deepens the commitment to implement what has been agreed on. A large and very influential group learns and adopts aspects of the scientific mindset by being part of its systematic use on real issues—action learning at its best.

The detailed planning of RME must produce a Consensus Day capable of significantly moving the dial; it must challenge, inspire, and accelerate organizational understanding and intimacy, while also delivering on the expectations created in the initial employee workshops. As Boston Scientific's employee representatives said in the Consensus Day wrap-up:

> "I'm one of nature's biggest skeptics, so if I believe in this anyone can believe in this."

> "Proud, privileged, honored to be a part of what we've done here over the last couple of days."

> "The best two days I've ever spent in work."

> "We need to mark the 11th and 12th of May 2015 because this is the start of the new Boston Scientific and a great place to work."

In the first few hours of Consensus Day, senior leaders, and others, become nervous and impatient as the hours go by with no apparent progress being made. Participants are learning, slowly at first, how to listen with an intent to understand, how to assume pos-itive intent, and how to reach consensus in such a large diverse and initially mistrustful group.

The facilitator must resist the pressure to quicken the pace as this would increase mistrust of the senior team and of the facilitator. Moving on too quickly also leaves behind those who need more time to reflect before making big decisions that impact everyone's future.

In setting expectations for Consensus Day, I describe the roller coaster of emotions and participants nod sagely in response; it is only when they experience the frustration, the hope, and the sense of achievement when they look up at the wall and see what has been decided in the room that they understand.

Be Cautious in Planning but Brave in Execution

When Consensus Day is coming to an end, I inform the participants that there is one more key task to complete. The powerful momentum that builds creates overcommitment; each commitment made is practical in isolation, but cumulatively these commitments lead to unrealistic expectations. At that point I ask what key organizational events are planned for the same periods as the work agreed on, and we review and relax the aggressiveness of target completion dates for projects. We also redistribute the workload, asking others to replace those who have volunteered for too many commitments. The principle is to be cautious in planning but brave and quick in execution.

Understand That Consensus Day Is Not the Only Option

The Consensus Day option is not always feasible for organizations. As an example, one factory had a totally aligned leadership team committed to implementing RME. Assessing risk and sustainability is part of the senior team Diagnostic Day, I asked about any anticipated changes in leadership or external impact on the site that would endanger mass engagement. The senior team discussed an upcoming corporate review of the manufacturing footprint across the world. It was too risky to march the workforce up to the top of the hill when there was a prospect of having to not only march them down again, but march some of them into unemployment. In that and similar cases, we applied the rejected premise principle and found an alternative approach.

Select External Facilitators Using RME Criteria

External facilitators who can operate large group decision-making events such as Consensus Day must have the capability to operate along the support-challenge continuum shown in Figure 12.1. Many can do the support side extremely well, and this is what is emphasized in conventional facilitation training; far fewer are willing to challenge their clients and prospective clients due to fear of endangering their future income. The external facilitator's ability and courage to challenge skillfully is essential to RME. This starts when working with the senior team to ensure rigorous scope while maximizing solution space and remains key throughout.

FIGURE 12.1 **Support-Challenge Continuum**

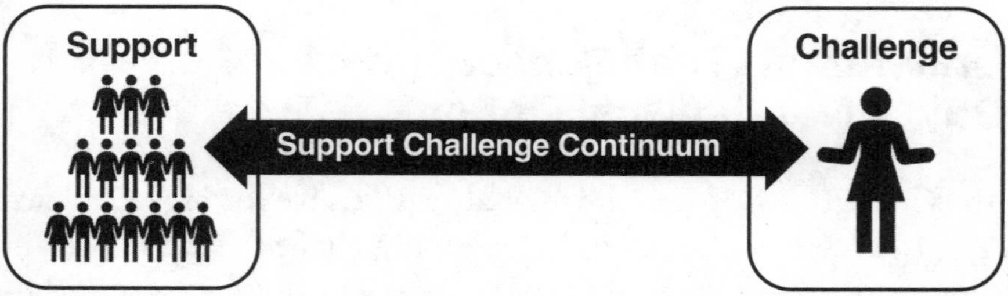

I have often told senior teams that their initial plans are unlikely to meet their objectives and that they need to strengthen the inputs to get the outputs they are seeking. This feedback is often unpalatable. My advice frequently necessitates senior leaders taking more personal risk and moving outside their individual and collective comfort zones and beyond their previous experiences. At this point the facilitator is not helping if they are too empathetic about your fears and insufficiently courageous to challenge your existing position. You need that challenge to achieve a better outcome consistent with your interests.*

The external facilitator requires a track record of successfully facilitating large groups to consensus, not mere compromise, in deeply contested issues.† As such, arbitration, mediation, and conciliation experience is valuable, but some facilitators only achieve compromise. It is crucial to test for a track record of reaching consensus in very large groups, in highly contested environments, with high levels of negative and limiting assumptions characterized by cynicism and lack of trust.

In unionized environments, the facilitator must understand, and have empathy for, how and why trade unions emerged in the nineteenth century. Key here is empathy for how RME, as a powerful form of direct engagement of an organization with its employees, is easily perceived as a threat to the indirect model of trade union representation.

When selecting facilitators, test for a track record of using a vigorous approach to data gathering, diagnostics, and problem solving. This capability will minimize the gaps between the collective but subjective diagnosis of diverse employee groups and the emergent data collected in the months after Consensus Day. This is key to

---

* For more about helping groups move from their initial positions to their interests see Fisher and Ury 1981.

† Search Conferences are an example; see Weisbord 1993.

sustaining the initial credibility of Consensus Day and the Joint Change Plan that is a key outcome of it.*

The facilitator must have a track record of gaining credibility quickly at all levels so that the bow wave effect starts in the early workshops and builds cumulatively into Consensus Day and beyond.

The facilitator must also be capable of managing the heightened emotion as a large Consensus Day group learns how to reach consensus in real time with high stakes. This must be done while patiently probing for understanding. The approach to consensus must be both data-literate and emotionally intelligent, allowing common ground to emerge organically rather than pressing for a decision prematurely. This is deeply frustrating for many leaders whose career advancement has been earned by a record of being decisive and getting things done quickly.

Finally, the facilitator needs expertise in how other organizations have successfully innovated to overcome similar obstacles to those prioritized by employees. The selection of who you trust to manage all these factors to a transformational conclusion is a key factor in the success of RME.

Have Your Employees Train Your Directors: Build Deep and Wide Internal Facilitation Capability

RME was designed to move the dial, to increase the quality and quantity of the services and goods that organizations provide to its stakeholders and to wider society. Removing risk-averse barriers to recruitment and promotion is a key lever. In every organization the latent capabilities of many employees lie dormant, invisible to management. Peer-group credible and highly skilled facilitators at all

---

* Tweaks will emerge through implementation, but as these are made by joint management-employee implementation groups, employee ownership of any changes is retained.

levels significantly increases the volume of adult-adult, commercially and emotionally literate conversations. Imagine the cumulative impact of those conversations on your organization's problem identification and solving, innovation, conflict prevention, and cognitive and social diversity.

Your competitors will struggle to match that level of improvement. If you operate in a noncommercial environment, imagine the impact on the quality and speed of the services you provide for your stakeholders. High-quality facilitation is a meta competency systematically leveraging all other activities an employee engages in. All other things being equal, organizations with skilled facilitators at every level and in every area will outperform those that do not have this capability.

Chapter 8 stressed the importance of signaling commitment to the new culture. What more powerful message could be sent about commitment to the new culture's nonhierarchical and opportunity-rich nature than having directors trained by highly skilled frontline employees?

Design Leadership Development Specifically to Sustain Engagement, Enablement, and a High-Performance Continuous Improvement Culture

Organizations tend to rely on existing, conventional leadership development programs to support their engagement and culture change efforts. I rarely see strict Pareto analysis used to focus and maximize the results. In contrast, applying the design criteria for leadership development outlined in Chapter 7 will systematically address the top four causes of suboptimization identified earlier. By applying these design criteria, your employees will see and feel the direct connection between their inputs and efforts and their leaders' skills and approaches, and you will reinforce existing improvement initiatives.

To avoid duplication and to gain permission to differentiate locally, some of my clients have negotiated exemptions from aspects of corporate leadership programs using the mutual recognition of standards approach. In effect, they augment corporate programs with the specific training designed to support RME. The latter matters for employees as it retains the explicit and transparent connection to the specific employee outputs from the initial employee workshops and this cannot be replicated by any centralized leadership program however good. This aids authenticity and ensures alignment between the three focus areas of engagement, leadership, and Continuous Improvement.

Corporate leadership programs are often of high quality and will cover much of the same headline topics but usually without the multiplier effects described earlier. They also include subjects that did not feature highly enough on the Pareto analysis of what was moving the dial. This has an accidentally dilutive effect similar to argument dilution in negotiation.

Focus, Don't Dilute

The Cathedral Higher Purpose Model (CHPM) is the outcome of a strict Pareto. The effect of applying Pareto is to de-emphasize several common management interventions, thus creating a powerful focused prioritization. It is important not to blunt this powerful prioritization by adding interventions, which although always well-intentioned, featured lower in the "does it move the dial enough?" test. Counterintuitively for some, "less is more" moves the dial further than "more is more."

The guidance for your external suppliers and learning and development providers is to discover, using data, what moves the dial and then deliver a small number of key interventions at high levels of quality and quantity, while assertively challenging noncore activities of all types. This challenge is particularly important when interventions of zero scientific validity become fashionable or are the panicked reaction to political events dominated by activist groups. These groups are not your friends; they have little empathy for, or understanding of, the day-to-day challenges of organizational life.* A bonus is this will reduce the overcommitment of your highest performers and prevent the demoralizing effect of working hard on nonimpactful interventions.

Remember the Dynamic Nature of the Cathedral Higher Purpose Model

The dynamic nature of the CHPM is crucial to maximizing results. Ensure that your leadership programs do not teach skills in isolation ignoring the multiple systems and leverage effects outlined earlier. This will also prevent predictable frustrations such as relying on recognition programs to increase the quantity of recognition when much more reliable routes exist to find and appreciate the hidden heroes discussed in Chapter 7 or the sometimes-dangerous confusion around when to coach and when to use constructive feedback.

Frame Leadership as a Contact Sport

The Quality × Quantity equation in the CHPM is crucial for results, therefore ensure that your leaders' span of control and leader standard work enables them to have sufficient opportunities for high-quality conversations. It doesn't matter how skilled your leaders are if they are not deploying their skills often enough with enough people.

---

* These groups see organizations as mere battlegrounds for their political agenda, which, by definition, will be divisive in any workforce.

Deploy End User–Focused Coaching and Make It a Common Good

When discussing producer capture, we saw how convenience for the service provider aligns with the best service for the user. Deploy a coaching approach that integrates data-literate diagnostics and problem-solving methodology. Ensure that coaching is not rationed by cost, and is never what economists call a scarce good but is always a common good, unrestricted by hierarchy. As the RME coaching approach is not costly to scale across your organization, finance will not be a limiting factor.

At a minimum, train every leader at every level not only how to be both a good opportunistic and set-piece coach, but also how to systematically leverage other RME skills across their multiple daily exchanges with colleagues.*

In summary, coaching needs to be flexible rather than prescriptive, and to be deployed in the end user–focused manner outlined in Chapter 7, rather than the producer captured, cost-rationed, and hierarchical versions commonly offered. It needs to supply the new opportunities that keep recognition fresh (see Chapter 7), undermine negative and limiting assumptions, be a laser spotlight on the common errors even the brightest people make, and provide a key role in developing all employees to the maximum of their potential.

Finally, coaching needs to be leveraged by the other skills in the CHPM and must not be delivered in a theoretical bubble of its own. That way it will move the dial.

Maximize Leverage

RME leverages employee engagement, leadership, and Continuous Improvement. These multiplier effects are cumulative, so failing to use one has a knock-on effect on the others. It is key is to maximize

---

* Training all employees how to coach is better; examples include Bacardi and ICBF.

these leverages. If the leverage opportunities are not all taken, it has the predictable consequences outlined in Chapter 10. If partial implementation is appropriate for your organization, minimize the failure to gain by deploying the rejected premise principle to focus your mitigation.

Build and Leverage Continuous Improvement Capability

When originally designing RME, I had a design concern. My fear was, what happens if, despite multiple design features aimed at scientific rigor,* the outcome of our collective diagnosis and problem-solving is scientifically inaccurate? What if we produce a mere subjective collection of lived experiences? We could create very powerful ownership, as designed, but of dangerously misguided, unscientific, and possibly counterproductive outcomes—what I call "owned idiocy"![†]

To prevent this, it is crucial to ensure adequate Continuous Improvement capability is available to the elected group on Consensus Day, and for the subsequent project management and data collection necessary to implement the decisions made. The planning for this starts at the senior team Diagnostic Day workshop.

It is important to ensure your Continuous Improvement capability (internal and external) is of sufficient quality to avoid frustrating the initial high engagement of employees with poor problem solving and project management implementation. In addition, validate, jointly with employees, the *qualitative* data produced by the initial employee workshops and by Consensus Day by robust quantitative data before implementation.

---

* Such as minimizing groupthink, systematically driving adult-adult conversations throughout the process, and insisting on verifiable evidence and data rather than assumptions and bias.
† I have sometimes used a less polite form of words.

Key is to develop the capability of the internal improvement team. For example, ensure the team deeply understands and operationalizes Deming's point (1982) that we need to analyze carefully what to focus our improvement efforts on, as he put it: "It is not enough to do your best; you must know what to do and then do your best."

This is just one of many ways in which the quality of the Continuous Improvement capability must be developed to leverage the engagement and enablement outcomes of RME. Another key area is to create what I call widespread analytical strength.

Build Widespread Analytical Strength but Understand the Limits of Analysis

It is often said that it is crucial to "speak with data." A more rounded principle is to "speak with data; but never trust it." We have seen how crucial coaching is to the CHPM. In the coaching training, having completed the diagnostic and problem-solving phases, I ask participants, with a grin:

> Now that we have thoroughly diagnosed what the issue is and thoroughly tested against the known greatest sources of diagnostic error and examined all possible ways forward against robust and ranked criteria, the solution that emerges must be foolproof, is that correct?

I work with bright people, and participants often respond with "what about known unknowns?" and, "even worse, unknown unknowns!" Both known unknowns and unknown unknowns limit the reliability of any analysis, however disciplined, knowledgeable, and bias- and noise-aware those conducting it are.*

---

* Kahneman, Sibony, and Sunstein (2021) argue: "It is very likely that intrinsic variability in the functioning of the brain also affects the quality of our judgments in ways that we cannot possibly hope to control."

We can't control this variability, but what we can do is identify the sources of error and then mitigate the malign effects. This is why I focus on memory-boosting design features such as fun, competitive quizzes, and all the other sustaining mechanisms (see Chapters 3, 5, 7, and 9).

All analysis is limited by these factors. Before implementing any solution, test it in practice. Develop methods of inexpensive experimentation and similar approaches such as including a category of decision in your decision-making menu assessed as "safe to try."* In addition, some things just can't be measured or counted, but they may be more important than other factors that can be. In such circumstances fiercely resist the temptation to make decisions based entirely on what can be measured.

Prevent Succession Planning Destroying the Employee-Created Culture

We saw in Chapter 8 how one site leader refused a big promotion because he knew that the person designated to succeed him lacked empathy for the culture that lay behind the site's outstanding performance. As he said: "I knew this would undermine years of what it took to get us here so I stayed put; it was the wrong decision for my career, but it was the right decision for all the people who had taken us through Covid; I couldn't leave them with a boss who didn't understand our culture. I can't pick my successor, but I will do everything in my power to influence my bosses and they are smart guys who have listened."

This leader understood the importance of getting the succession right. This is not universal. There is an understandable desire by individuals to move up the organization. The damage done by insensitive new leaders preoccupied by leaving their mark rather

---

* A decision-making menu prevents the natural tendency to passively drift into using your preferred decision-making method in circumstances when that method is unsuitable such as looking for consensus when consensus is not required.

than appreciating what they have inherited is immense. It is also feeds the very cynicism RME removes. The experiences leaders have of Consensus Day and the weeks surrounding it create emotional commitment to RME. This cannot be present to the same degree in new leaders joining the organization. This has important sustainability consequences especially for the successor in the most senior role. This can be managed very well, for example Boston Scientific has repeatedly ensured that successors in key roles were powerful RME advocates who modeled and referenced their Behavioral Standards and leadership values in their day-to-day work. This sent powerful messages about the continued commitment of senior leaders to the employee-owned culture.

Succession planning features in the RME senior team Diagnostic Day because succession issues are fatal if not handled well. Ensure that your talent management approach gives sustaining a strong culture substantial weight and provides creative alternatives to promotion for key leaders.

Design Multiple Systematic Sustaining Mechanisms

Let's look at Phase 4 of this process shown in Figure 12.2. In Chapter 9 we saw how to sustain the culture change via a bespoke leadership approach and internal facilitators for both the Behavioral Standards and leadership.* The methodology for creating Behavioral Standards includes a Behavioral Standard that sustains all the others: ensure your team understands that methodology and the philosophy that underpins it. Similarly, nurture a Continuous Improvement and scientific mindset to build repeatedly on gains rather than become complacent. In summary, deploy multiple sustaining mechanisms to prevent the new culture stalling.

---

* These facilitators are trained to develop additional local sustaining mechanisms to retain freshness and promote innovation and fun.

FIGURE 12.2 **Changing System and Culture Simultaneously**

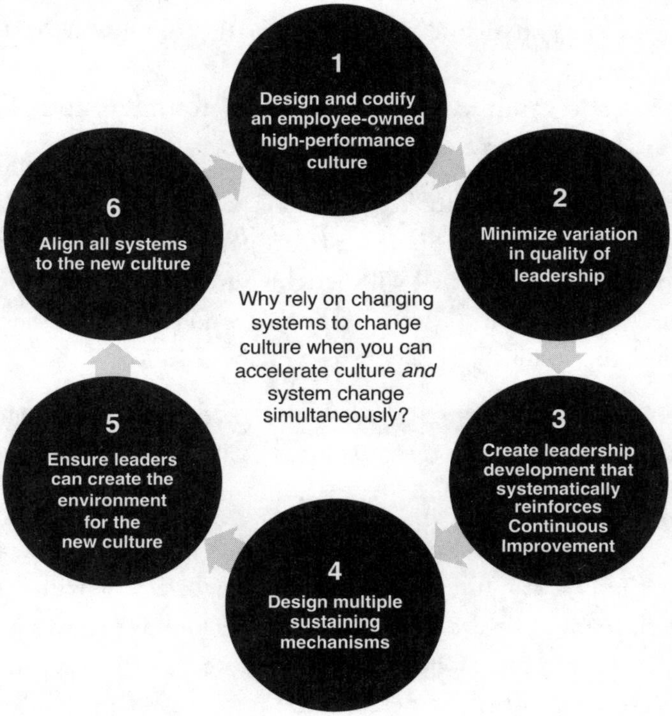

Why rely on changing systems to change culture when you can accelerate culture *and* system change simultaneously?

1
Design and codify an employee-owned high-performance culture

2
Minimize variation in quality of leadership

3
Create leadership development that systematically reinforces Continuous Improvement

4
Design multiple sustaining mechanisms

5
Ensure leaders can create the environment for the new culture

6
Align all systems to the new culture

Recruit and Promote on Traits

In Chapter 7 we saw how erecting artificial barriers to entry both limits the pool of talent from which your organization can recruit and has unintended negative consequences regarding diversity, especially social and cognitive diversity. There is another way. The Timpson Group successfully recruit prisoners. Its chairman, James Timpson, explained his experience:

> It's better to put in the hard yards and look for people from all walks of life, even if they have imperfect CVs. They just need the two things we love but can't always find . . . energy

and personality. Most of our recruits never actually filled out a CV . . . we can train anyone to cut keys and repair shoes, but we can't change someone's personality. (Timpson 2021)

Other leaders agree. Herb Kelleher, founder and CEO of Southwest Airlines, had a similar approach to recruitment. He said:

Anyone who likes to be called a "professional" probably shouldn't be around Southwest Airlines . . . we want people who can do things well with laughter and grace . . . we look for . . . people with a sense of humor who don't take themselves too seriously. (Freiberg and Freiberg 1996)

When *Harvard Business Review* analyzed the heroic reaction of the hotel staff during the terrorist attack on the Mumbai Taj Hotel, the authors noted:

Contrary to popular perception, the Taj Group doesn't scout for the best English speakers or math whizzes; it will even recruit would-be dropouts. Its recruiters look for three character traits: respect for elders (how does he treat his teachers?); cheerfulness (does she perceive life positively even in adversity?); and neediness (how badly does his family need the income from a job?). (Deshpande and Raina 2011)

All these organizations recruit and promote on traits, and all have found talent in places where many organizations are not even looking. Look for it and you also will find it.

Confront the Soft Bigotry of Low Expectations

In my career, I always encouraged as much interaction as possible between schools and workplaces. I knew the opportunities available for kids with the right traits, and I wanted them to aim high for a career rather than the series of dead-end jobs I had at the start of my own working life. In 1984, Birds Eye Wall's was one of the highest paying employers in Kirkby—a deprived but vibrant community outside Liverpool with very high unemployment, especially for men. Birds Eye Wall's was then part of Unilever, so life-changing opportunities existed outside the local factory. During a visit from local kids, I got a call from a first line supervisor. He said "Frank, please come and stop the teacher demoralizing the students."

I rushed to the factory floor where the factory tour was continuing. I asked the supervisor what had been said, and he told me that the teacher had told the kids: "Remember this is where you will be if you do badly in your exams."

In the teacher's mind, working in a technically sophisticated factory was something for people who did badly at school. She was ignorant of the many scientists and engineers who make their careers in a company such as Unilever. For her, the private sector was an alien world where evil profit-making people exploited employees and not somewhere the children should aspire to work. Both Dyson (2021) and Birbalsingh (2020) explain the damage these attitudes have done to children's life chances. Both provide inspirational alternatives aligned with the thinking in these pages.

The phrase "the soft bigotry of low expectations" was coined by President George W. Bush in 2000 in a speech to the National Association for the Advancement of Colored People. It marked the launching of the No Child Left Behind Act. This bigotry is tragically common in both education and organizational life.

As Birbalsingh* and her teachers have argued, "it is not 'kind' to lower standards and expectations in misplaced empathy for children from disadvantaged backgrounds; this kindness condemns children to a cold blast of reality when entering a real world that does not 'make allowances'" (Birbalsingh 2020).

Teachers such as Birbalsingh love their pupils, but their kindness is to prepare children to overcome the challenges reality will impose

---

* Head teacher in an unselective school in a deprived area in London that has out-performed selective and expensive private schools.

on them when they leave school; part of how they do this is to insist on standards and rigor in learning and behavior; expectations are high, and her school delivers on them. They call their approach "warm/strict." How is this relevant to RME?

As HR director, I visited a factory in what might be called "the wrong side of town." As I was taken around the factory, I remarked to the plant director that he must be proud that we had provided so many well-paid jobs in a deprived community. He laughed and replied: "Frank, we don't recruit anyone from this side of the city." I asked a number of questions such as "What happens to applications from this side of the city?"; "What routes to promotion are available to high performers who lack formal qualifications?"; "What career paths are available into technician roles and from technician into engineering?"; and "What work is done in local schools to raise expectations, of both teachers and students, of what can be achieved in a career in manufacturing?" The answers were deeply uninspiring and, more importantly, I was informed that no one had ever asked questions like these before. My boss subsequently received feedback that my behavior was overassertive and had created unease among the senior team.

Imagine if the senior team had been able to escape the low expectations it had of an entire community? Imagine the impact of providing well-paid jobs and career progression to members of that community? Imagine how much employee engagement could have been created?

The plant director and his senior team saw me as naive or maybe even mad; they appreciated that the union issues I had come to address were resolved, but I saw no evidence that my questions had encouraged any change in attitude. This team had not been recruited on traits, and there was a palpable disconnect in values. The factory closed a few years later.

That well-educated but imaginatively challenged senior team saw the local community as a hostile foreign land that they drove into and away from every day without touching the sides; I recommend you embrace your local communities and keep your factories open. One way of doing this is to ensure you are aware of the capabilities of your existing employees and the communities surrounding your locations.

Focus on What Employees Can Do, Not on What They Can't

It is crucial for leaders to know and build on the capabilities that employees demonstrate outside of work. In addition, as we saw earlier, recruiting and promoting on traits prevents the exclusion of excellent candidates by job requirements that are too narrow and indirectly discriminate against groups from disadvantaged backgrounds.

When I train internal facilitators, the internal role advertisement does not specify specific skills or formal qualifications. An example from a RME location states:

Effective facilitators:
- Have immense desire to learn
- Have genuine interest in and desire for others to learn and reach their potential
- Show appreciation of the efforts of others
- Are willing, always, to take initiative to make things better
- Show a strong drive for Continuous Improvement as demonstrated by actions at work or outside work
- Show courage in defending people or groups when they are being criticized behind their backs
- Lead by example so they can take the training out of the classroom and make it a reality at work
- Maintain a positive spirit when things don't go well

Remember the discussions in the Engagement Workshop on human potential. No prior skills or formal qualifications are required so do not be put off by any previous bad learning experiences at school or at work—this will be different; we will build on your existing strengths, not try to create 12 identical robots!

In summary, discover the capabilities you already have hidden in your organization, meet employees where they are, be empathetic to variation in life opportunities, but don't reduce expectations. Remember academic qualifications are just one form of capability, and remember there are many other capabilities in a workforce that are hugely relevant to creating a high-performance culture.

Agree on Locally Owned Behavioral Standards

Behavioral Standards are owned by employees, they are infused with local language and identity, and they rapidly change previously perceived limits to what is possible. Corporate values, when implemented well, are important integrative mechanisms. Behavioral Standards are differentiators (see Chapter 6). Ensure your organization balances both, thus harnessing the power and energy of local ownership in support of your values and culture change.

Look for the Best in Human Nature

Unfair negative judgments made about people and their capability feature in RME employee data again and again. Typical was a lady with a stammer who told her RME workshop, "Throughout my life, people have assumed I am stupid; it hurts; it hurts every time." That vivid language resonated with the entire site when it was included in the feedback. It was addressed in the Behavioral Standards.

Everywhere we have implemented RME, employees have spoken movingly about what it feels like for others to make negative assumptions about them. This tendency has been amplified by the cruel and uncharitable way in which people are abused on social media for daring to hold opinions that differ from those of their abusers. Key to success in implementing RME is to robustly move in the opposite direction and look for the best in people.

If you look for things to criticize in others, you will find them, because good people make mistakes. Look for the best in others, and you will not have difficulty finding it.

Kill Boredom

As we saw in Chapter 11, memorability matters. Curiosity, stories, vivid language, and humor makes things memorable and life worth living. Boredom and lack of passion will destroy your culture change, damage your talent attraction, and severely limit the learning of your organization.

Cognitive diversity matters but has its limits, so gently and gradually more robustly challenge, and if every effort fails, remove from your organization the humor-bypassed, risk-averse, glum, statistically illiterate, catastrophizing, high-maintenance experts on what can't be done.

Better still, get them jobs with your competitors!

Protect Your High Performers and Ensure Your Process Has Teeth

Many designers of employee engagement surveys assume that high employee turnover is an indication of low engagement. RME locations tend to score very well in these surveys, but some would have been even higher if this assumption was not so prevalent among engagement survey providers.

In one RME, many employees had been recruited not on traits but by poor, interview-only processes. Because of this poor recruitment, an unusually high 6 percent of the entire workforce did not meet the standards required in the new culture and didn't respond to help. The Escalation part of the CHPM was invoked, and they were removed from the business with empathy and strong support to obtain jobs elsewhere. It was important to avoid perverse incentives and to make accountability transparent, so no payoffs were used. Despite this high rate of dismissals, due to the scrupulously fair escalation process, all challenges to third-party fair employment mechanisms found in favor of the organization. The significant help given to find alternative jobs was both the right thing to do and explicitly acknowledged that the individuals were not responsible for the poor recruitment used to employ them. Employee engagement scores improved year on year.

How was it possible that the dismissal of 6 percent of a workforce, including managers, coincided with a rapid and sustained increase in employee engagement? Consider who suffers most when some team members do not contribute their fair share of the workload of a team. The workforce saw a respectful and fair process involving opportunities to change behavior. When those who refused to contribute equitably to a team's workload were removed, team morale and performance increased. Once that process was complete, turnover reduced significantly, and the site was no longer penalized in engagement surveys.

Let's consider a counter-factual: What would have happened if the site had only operated the left side of the CHPM, using only recognition and coaching but avoiding difficult conversations with those who were underperforming? What do you anticipate is the effect on the most hardworking employees and on team cohesion when they see others contributing much less and thus increasing the workload of those already carrying a disproportionate workload?

Managers often avoid these performance conversations. Having listened to tens of thousands of employees describe what frustrates them most at work, the easiest way for an individual leader to lose the respect of the team is to fail to deal with low performance and the resultant inequitable work distribution. How to avoid this and ensure true high-performance teamwork is part of the CHPM training.

Employees understand this better than many designers of surveys. They understand that some turnover, like some cholesterol and some stress, is good, and turnover per se is not an indication of low engagement. In this factory, *initially* high turnover was the consequence of poor recruitment remedied by the subsequent application of standards and accountability. This can happen in the early years after a radical culture change process such as RME and before rigorous recruitment and probation processes are introduced.

Increase Employees' Standard of Living in Innovative Ways

In the initial employee workshops, we are frequently informed, "Don't bother with all this stuff, just increase everyone's pay." Employees are simply repeating the "throw more money at it" lazy thinking common among those who don't understand that wealth must be created before it can be redistributed. As pay is often a matter determined by a negotiating process between unions and management or between individuals and their employer, it is usually out of scope in RME. RME has, however, increased standards of living.

Outcomes from RME that have increased employees' standard of living without increasing general wages include creating a transparent and employee-driven shift change process that enabled couples to reduce or eliminate childcare costs. In addition, systematically removing artificial barriers to progression resulted in widespread increases in promotions. Given the post-tax increase in disposable income that outcomes like this created, this had a much greater impact on standard of living than multiple years of pay raises in a period of low inflation.

In addition, addressing span of control has created new roles and provided shorter routes to management positions. In turn, this facilitated those previously seen as unqualified for management positions having successful careers in leadership, some reaching very senior roles.*

---

* This has happened despite the qualification inflation trend holding others back in rival organizations to the competitive advantage of the organizations who have had the courage to buck this trend.

To conclude, ensure your organization has an opportunity-oriented improvement culture, owned by its own employees, with systematic skilled coaching and problem solving at all levels; the resultant boost to innovation will create increases in employees' standard of living independent of wages.

Invest in Success and Make It Transparent

We saw in Chapter 5 how corporate leaders in DePuy (Johnson & Johnson) and Boston Scientific responded to rapid performance gains in their local sites by trusting the sites with new and more and more complex and value-adding products and services.

When corporate leaders make decisions to transparently allocate scarce capital resources to far-away locations that have delivered for their customers, this adds to the commercial literacy of the workforce and creates a leveraged success loop. Employees see the investment, the jobs, the effect on their careers, and the opportunities for their communities. Skeptics become converts and add their weight to the culture change. All of this is cumulative and reinforces the Higher Purpose of RME.

Some organizations have different models for allocating investment; if yours is one of those, I recommend you examine the opportunity cost of your current system and move toward the high transparency, high accountability model outlined here.

Oppose Crony Capitalism

In Chapter 2, we discussed how to meet employee yearning for purpose at work. Part of that effort is to help people become aware of a better form of capitalism than the "Too Big to Fail" and "Too Big to Jail" crony capitalism featured so often in films and news. Left and right of the political continuum, we must unite in opposition to crony capitalism in all its forms such as producer capture, regulatory capture, monopoly (public and private), rent-seeking, all of it! Just like opposing racism, opposing this distorted form of capitalism is something we can unite on, provided we discuss these issues in the spirit of assuming positive intent outlined in these pages. Crucial also is learning from the story of the old and young fish.

The story goes that old fish passes two young fish swimming in the opposite direction. He acknowledges them and asks, "How's the water today?"

They are bemused by the question and swim on. After a while one looks at the other and asks: "What is water?"

Just like the young fish not appreciating the role of water in their life, it is important that we avoid taking the freedoms and responsibilities of liberal democracy for granted. Similarly, we must help people understand that ethical capitalism exists (see Mackey and Sisodia 2013). It can be created by genuine rapid and mass engagement led by leaders with values to match. I hope you are one of those leaders and that this book helps you achieve great things for your organization, your family, and your community. If it does, my purpose for writing this book will be fulfilled.

Finally let's circle back to the start of the book in the Postscript.

Postscript

In the Preface I mentioned the lesson I learned as a four-year-old when my mother said to me: "Don't see the lady as a cleaner, darling. See the lady as a lady who is doing a cleaning job at the moment."

My mother helped again during Becton Dickinson's RME in 2012. At the end of Consensus Day, at about 12:30 am, a group of employees and I assembled in the bar of the Fitzpatrick Castle Hotel. After a few drinks, one of the employees pulled out a letter to *The Irish Times* from early November 2011. This was four months before the RME process began. He explained he had been covering a step in the line in early November when he saw that day's *Irish Times* letters' page open, and he read it. He saw a letter that had moved him, so he asked the operator if he could have the newspaper after the operator was finished with it. He took out the letter and showed it to me (Figure 13.1).

FIGURE 13.1 **My Mother's Role in BD's Consensus Day**

Letters to the Editor

The kindness of strangers

Sir, – I buried my mother in Dublin last week.

Her quality of life had become poor over her last two years as she struggled to overcome the effects of smoking on her eyesight, lungs and heart.

But the people of Dublin noticed and did not stand back: bus drivers on the 75 and 16A routes got out of their buses and walked her across to her little apartment in Nutgrove Court; some even helped her up the steps and into her little home. Three complete strangers, her "three angels", did her shopping, her washing, her ironing, took her to get her silver hair done every week and took her on her more frequent, but always reluctant (for her), visits to her doctor and hospi-

tals. Her local pharmacy in Rathfarnham let her rest in the shop and often took her across to the bus stop or arranged a lift home.

We had a lovely last day and we changed our plans to bring her over to me in the UK, (she was only doing that to make it easy for me) and she said, "I don't want to die in England". She went to sleep happy with that decision and did not wake up.

Thank you so much to the many random strangers who did so much for my mother at her time of need. To those I know, I have shown, and will always show, my appreciation; this letter is also for those I do not know. – Yours, etc,

FRANK DEVINE,
Fennyland Lane, Kenilworth,
Warwickshire, England.

He told me that, during the early RME employee workshops, some colleagues had questioned my sincerity. His answer was, "No, this guy is for real. He means it about reducing forced emigration from Ireland. Read this," while showing them my letter.

Ironically, my mum had been excited in September 2011 when I told her about the BD process as the site's location, Dun Laoghaire, meant I would come home to her each evening after the workshops and be with her for more than two weeks. The process started in February 2012, and sadly she died on November 1, 2011; but she did help me via my letter of thanks to the kind strangers who saw her struggles and acted to help, and the kind BD Consensus Day representative who noticed the letter and used it to such good effect.

References

Berne, E. (1964). *Games People Play: The Psychology of Human Relationships*. Grove Press.

Bastos, A., and C. Sharman (2019). *Strat to Action*. McGraw Hill.

Birbalsingh, K. (2020). *The Power of Culture*. John Catt Educational Ltd.

Brophy, A. (2012). *Lean: How to Streamline Your Organization, Engage Employees and Create a Competitive Edge*. Financial Times Series.

Burke, E. (1790). *Reflections on the Revolution in France*. James Dodsley.

Campbell, A., M. Devine, and D. Young (1990). *A Sense of Mission*. Economist Publications/Hutchinson.

Carroll, L. (1865). *Through the Looking Glass*. Macmillan and Co.

Chambers, S. (2022). Prufrock diary section. *Sunday Times*. June 12.

Chivers, T., and D. Chivers (2021). *How to Read Numbers*. Weidenfeld & Nicolson.

Collins, J. (2001). *Good to Great: Why Some Companies Make the Leap . . . and Others Don't*. Harper Collins.

Deming, W. E. (1982). *Out of the Crisis*. The MIT Press Cambridge.

Dennis, P. (2006). *Getting the Right Things Done*. Lean Enterprise Institute.

Deshpande, R., and A. Raina (December 2011). "The Ordinary Heroes of the Taj." *Harvard Business Review*.

De Smet, A., B. Dowling, M. Mugayar-Baldocchi, and B. Schaninger (September 2021). " 'Great Attrition' or 'Great Attraction'? The Choice Is Yours." *McKinsey Quarterly*.

Devine, F. (2001). *Report of the Bacardi-Martini Pay and Job Evaluation Working Party*. Bacardi internal document.

Devine, F., and J. Bicheno (2019). "Creating Employee 'Pull' for Improvement: Rapid, Mass Engagement for Sustained Lean." Proceedings from the 6th Lean Educators Conference 2019. Springer.

Dockery, K. (2009). *Special Warfare, Special Weapons*. The Emperor's Press.

Dror, I. E. (2020). "Cognitive and Human Factors in Expert Decision Making: Six Fallacies and the Eight Sources of Bias." *Analytical Chemistry*.

Dyson, J. (2021). *Invention: A Life*. Simon & Schuster.

Fisher and Ury (1981). *Getting to Yes*. Houghton Mifflin.

FitzGerald, G. (1973). *Towards a New Ireland*. Torc Press.

Freiberg, K., and J. Freiberg (1996). *Nuts! Southwest Airlines' Crazy Recipe for Business and Personal Success*. Bard Press.

Gallup (2022). "How to Measure Employee Engagement with the Q12." https://www.gallup.com/workplace/356063/gallup-q12 -employee-engagement-survey.aspx?msclkid=05389c47d16b1c8a 9f52ff3db4c6d249&utm_source=bing&utm_me

Garvey, P. (2015). "Engaging an Organization in Operational Excellence: A Case Study in Mass Engagement." MSc Dissertation, University of Buckingham.

Gitsham, M. (2009). *Developing the Global Leader of Tomorrow*. Ashridge Business School.

Hauser, J. R., and D. Clausing (May 1988). "The House of Quality." *Harvard Business Review*.

Herzog, S., and R. Hertwig (2014). "Think Twice and Then: Combining or Choosing in Dialectical Bootstrapping?" *Journal of Experimental Psychology*.

Hofstede, G., G. J. Hofstede, and M. Minkow (2010). *Cultures and Organizations*. McGraw Hill.

Imai, M. (1986). *Kaizen: The Key to Japan's Competitive Success.* McGraw Hill.

Ioannidis, J. P. A. (2005). "Why Most Published Research Findings Are False." *PLoS Med* 2(8): e124.

Johansen, B. (2020). *Full-Spectrum Thinking: How to Escape Boxes in a Post-Categorical Future.* Institute for the Future.

Kahneman, D. (2011). *Thinking, Fast and Slow.* Farrar, Strauss and Giroux.

Kahneman, D., O. Sibony, and C. Sunstein (2021). *Noise.* William Collins Books.

Kirwan, B. (1994). *A Guide to Practical Human Reliability Assessment.* Taylor & Francis.

Koenigsaecker, G. (2009). *Leading the Lean Enterprise Transformation.* Productivity Press.

Lawrence, P. R., and J. W. Lorsch (1986). *Organization and Environment: Managing Differentiation and Integration.* Harvard Business School Classics.

Lencioni, P. (2002). *The Five Dysfunctions of a Team.* Jossey-Bass.

Liker, J. (2004). *The Toyota Way.* McGraw Hill.

Mackey, J., and R. Sisodia (2013). *Conscious Capitalism: Liberating the Heroic Spirit of Business.* Harvard Business School Publishing Corporation.

Nielsen, C., and N. McCullough (May 2018). "How People Analytics Can Help You Change Process, Culture, and Strategy." *Harvard Business Review.*

Popper, K. (1972). *The Logic of Scientific Discovery.* Hutchinson.

Rother, M. (2010). *Toyota Kata: Managing People for Improvement, Adaptiveness, and Superior Results.* McGraw Hill.

Rowntree, S. (1901). *Poverty: A Study of Town Life.* MacMillan.

Seddon, J. (2009). *Culture Change Is Free.* Quality World.

Syed, M. (2017). *The Greatest: The Quest for Sporting Perfection.* Hodder and Stoughton.

Syed, M. (2020). *Rebel Ideas.* John Murray Publishers.

Syed, M. (2021). "Our Economy Is Increasingly Sick." *Sunday Times*, March 4.

Tata Group Publications (2008). *Business of Excellence*. Group Publications.

Timpson, J. (2021). "My Lightbulb Moment: Recruit When You Don't Need To." *Sunday Times*, April 18.

Trist, E. (1981). *The Evolution of Socio-Technical Systems: A Conceptual Framework and an Action Research Program*. Ontario Ministry of Labour.

Twomey, W. (2011). "Beneath the Waterline: A Study of the Effect of Applying Leader Standard Work to the Social Aspects of a Manufacturing System on the Performance of the System." MSc Dissertation. Lean Enterprise Research Centre, Cardiff University.

Weisbord, M. A. (1993). *Discovering Common Ground*. Berrett-Koehler Publishers.

Wickens, P. (1987). *The Road to Nissan*. Macmillan.

Wilson, J. Q., and George L. Kelling (March 1982). "Broken Windows." *The Atlantic Monthly*.

Wolfe, M. (2019). "Capitalism. It's Time for a Reset." *Financial Times*, September 18.

Whyte, P. (2011). "Exploring the Use of Systems Thinking to Understand and Plan Change." MSc Dissertation. Lean Enterprise Research Centre, Cardiff University.

Index

Page numbers followed by *f* indicate figures; page numbers followed by *t* indicate tables.

About the Author

Frank Devine specializes in elite-level performance often via creating employee buy-in or "pull" for continuous improvement. He has lectured on master's programs at the Universities of Cardiff, Buckingham, and Warwick. His work has been tested in hundreds of sites and across every continent. His corporate career began at Shell and continued via major change initiatives in Unilever, Alvis, ABB, Fiat, and CMB before establishing his culture change consultancy in 1996. He also assesses soccer players for Ireland's underage international teams and was a UK parliamentary candidate in 1987. He is proud to be an honorary lifetime member of Warwick University's Jewish Society despite having no religious or family links to that tradition!